MINI TO MEGA TSUNAMI

Smyth & Helwys Publishing, Inc.
6316 Peake Road
Macon, Georgia 31210-3960
1-800-747-3016
©2024 by Ron Crawford
All rights reserved.

Library of Congress Cataloging-in-Publication Data

Names: Crawford, Ronald W., author.
Title: Mini to mega tsunami : a healthier perspective on grief / by Ron
Crawford.
Description: Macon, GA : Smyth & Helwys Publishing, [2024] | Includes
bibliographical references.
Identifiers: LCCN 2024038452 | ISBN 9781641735773 (paperback)
Subjects: LCSH: Grief--Religious aspects--Baptists. |
Bereavement--Religious aspects--Baptists. | Consolation.
Classification: LCC BV4909 .C74 2024 | DDC 248.8/6--dc23/eng/20240911
LC record available at https://lccn.loc.gov/2024038452

Advance Praise for *Mini to Mega Tsunami*

If you have ever wondered exactly what grief should look like, Ron Crawford's book dismantles many of the assumed patterns in favor of a nuanced approach. He combines research from the historical grief studies alongside religious and cultural expectations to develop a more thorough perspective. He uses his personal experience of the loss of his wife as well as his years of pastoral ministry to offer insights into what he has seen and witnessed as most helpful and harmful. This work will leave you hopeful that there is no one-size-fits-all method to correctly grieve while also offering helpful tools to guide us in our grief journeys.

— Dr. Melissa Fallen
Pastor, Glen Allen Baptist Church
Glen Allen, Virginia

In dealing with his own grief, C. S. Lewis said, "I thought I could describe a state; make a map of sorrow. Sorrow, however, turns out to be not a state but a process." In this book on grief, Ron Crawford affirms that sentiment. Reflecting on his experience of loss and grief Crawford offers an accessible framework for understanding one's experiences of grief—a process that one must process in one's one ways and in one's own timeline.

—Israel Galindo
Associate Dean for Lifelong Learning
Columbia Theological Seminary

I can't believe I'm about to use the word refreshing when speaking of a book on grief, but I believe that's the right word to use. In *Mini to Mega Tsunami: A Healthier Perspective on Grief*, Ron Crawford presents a refreshingly compassionate approach to understanding grief. Rather than relying on traditional models or stages of grief, he likens the experience to a tsunami, which varies in its intensity and its impact. Ron's draws on his experience—as a minister, as an educator of ministers, and as one who has walked the path of grief himself—and graciously and supportively offers to walk alongside us as we seek to make sense of our own grief and find hope in the process.

— *Rev. Dr. Daniel E. Glaze*
Pastor, River Road Church
Richmond, Virginia

In *Mini to Mega Tsunami*, Ron offers us a model for grief that is analytical, practical, and deeply personal. Many know the pain that comes with the death of a spouse, but few in life are able to make such a helpful recipe out of their own tragedy. Part primer, part reference manual, part memoir—I am thankful to finally have a book on grief that I can put in a congregant's hand before they might need it.

— *Rev. Dan Schumacher*
Senior Pastor, First Baptist Church
Colorado Springs, Colorado

Dr. Crawford (Ron) answered many questions I have struggled with so long surrounding grief. Grief and other emotions get bound together and are hard to unravel on our own. The brain work, including the work related to epigenetics, and the call to action at the book's conclusion were particularly impactful. As a local church pastor, I plan to encourage my parishioners to carry their grief with them, find and celebrate a new normal, and walk through their grief with both action and patience.

— *Rev. John H. Uldrick*
Senior Pastor, First Baptist Church Greenwood
Greenwood, South Carolina

Ron Crawford's manuscript arrived in my mailbox the week my mother passed away. While it took me a while to pick it up, it turned out to be a providential help and guide to my grief pathway. Crawford has combined his academic, ministerial, and first-person experiences to create a healthy and innovative approach to the tsunami of grief. I heartily commend it to anyone willing to see their grief as a mystery to be explored and embraced.

— *Bill Wilson*
Founding Director, The Center for Healthy Churches
Greenville, South Carolina

RON CRAWFORD

MINI TO MEGA
TSUNAMI

A HEALTHIER
PERSPECTIVE
ON GRIEF

Also by *Ron Crawford*

Finding Love Later in Life
Brunch at the Crooked Oak Café

Towel and Basin Memoir
Personal Reflections on Baptist Theological Seminary at
Richmond (co-editor)

Contents

Introduction

I am finally getting around to writing my book on grief; I must have started and stopped a dozen or more times. Each time I began the book, I was inspired by some article, comment, or memory regarding my own grief. And each time, I thought postponing the endeavor was the better path. It seems now is the "ripe" time for me to complete this long-anticipated project.

What is different this time around? Perspective. Personal grief is characterized by heights and valleys of emotion and thought. Through the roller-coaster ride of grief, it takes a while to achieve a sense of balance and find a new normal that is sunny and sometimes partly cloudy instead of overcast with loss. It has been seven years since the death of my wife, my high school sweetheart.

For those who have experienced significant loss, getting to a "new normal" and gaining "a sense of balance" is a big deal. I was ready to write a book about grief at the second anniversary of my wife's death. At the time, I thought I was achieving a sense of balance, but my first efforts at writing a book illustrated a different reality. That earlier attempt was focused on me, myself and I. It was a paltry effort to offer insights about grief while still struggling with my own deep emotions of profound grief. It takes a while—sometimes a good long while—before a sense of balance returns.

Even though I mentioned "seven years," I am not suggesting my timetable for finding a "new normal" is average or even desirable. I am simply noting it took me this long. Over these seven-plus years, I wrestled with two different struggles: one emotional, one intellectual.

The emotional struggle was more obvious: crying, sadness, cascading memories, and feeling emotional for no apparent reason. At times, my emotions seemed driven by subconscious issues I was completely unaware of and power-less to corral. I can't possibly recite all the times over the years I talked to a random stranger about the weather, politics, or nothing in particular and found an emotional lump in my throat, rendering me momentarily speechless. It is frustrating to get emotional when suggesting "Tomorrow will be warm." Even so, that seems to be the nature of grief.

My intellectual struggle was more subtle. It was focused on finding a metaphor or way of speaking about grief that was intellectually honest and true to my experience. Of course, there is no lack of information, myths, biases, and untruths in modern American society about the topic of grief. This general misinformation can complicate grief. I offer a few examples.

Nine weeks after my wife's death, I happened to see a friend for the first time after her death; he was out of the country when she died and did not attend the funeral. So, we saw each other by chance. We hugged, and I said, "It is great to see you."

He responded with, "So, how are you *really* doing?"

That particular day, I was feeling much better. The over-cast skies of grief had parted slightly for a moment, and I felt more like my old self. I replied, "I am doing great!"

I will never forget his reaction: horror filled his face. It was apparent he expected me to still be down in the doldrums of grief. I imagined him thinking, "How dare you feel great. Your wife just died!" My friend had expectations about my grief and how I should feel. Not conforming to his expectations created a sense of alarm for him.

Similar experiences prodded me to develop a strategy to deal with people when they engaged me in a conversation. I would evaluate their nonverbal cues and tone of voice to understand what they wanted me to say before I spoke. I would then ignore my thoughts and go with whatever I thought they wanted me to say. If in doubt, I would offer an innocuous, "Lots of ups and downs." It's sad to say, but I became pretty good at disguising my true feelings and offering up what I thought people wanted to hear. Better to be dishonest than to have friends chide me with silent facial expressions.

Another example: after the death of your spouse, when do you take your wedding band off?

Some people have pretty clear ideas about how long the wedding band should stay in place. I gave this topic a good bit of thought. The primary issue for me was when I wanted to deal with the potential resistance of friends. When it might be helpful in my journey with grief was a secondary consideration. Three months after my wife's death, my grown children were coming for a weekend to help me go through her things and decide what to save for the grandchildren and what to donate to a worthy cause. I took the wedding band off before their arrival, primarily to see if the ring's absence created issues for them. It was not raised as an issue by any of my children, so I left the ring on the nightstand beside my bed for several months.

The opinions, biases, and misinformation in American society make grief more difficult and complex.

My intellectual struggles settled in a more comfortable place around a few terms or concepts: profound grief (more to come later), the tsunami metaphor, and reclaiming a healthy future (a new normal); all central ideas in this book.

In selecting tsunami as the central metaphor to talk about grief, I am willingly and gladly abandoning the notion grief has stages, an idea entrenched in modern American culture. Grief, a highly personal experience, does not follow a linear or specific pathway. While the five stages of grief have taken on a life of their own in modern American culture, there simply is no generic pathway through it. The notion of stages through which individuals will travel in processing grief is not substantiated in clinical studies and establishes arbitrary, and at times harmful, norms for individuals experiencing it.

Tsunami is a much better metaphor. I selected tsunami as the central metaphor in this book for several reasons. First, it is an international term. Second, tsunami avoids the stages an individual must/may progress through. Third, tsunamis provide a helpful way to talk about different degrees of trauma in grief. Tsunamis come in various sizes (intensities), from mild to mega-tsunamis. Each size will require a different remedy for recovery: a mild tsunami may become an issue between a resident and an insurance company—provided the resident has appropriate insurance coverage. Or, in the case of a severe tsunami, a community-wide or national response may be in order.

I also wanted to provide a general book on grief that touched on the new science of bereavement. Brain research on grief is in its infancy but offers insights that need to be valued and woven into more holistic perspectives on grief. In this book, I am attempting to widen the conversation about grief and bring a more holistic perspective.

In writing this book, I simply want to share my journey and insights gained along the way. I hope that some of what I offer in this book will be helpful to others. I am not suggesting my experience and ideas are normative, right, or better. With grief, we all find our own way through the maze.

I am offering this book to save another fellow traveler some heartache along the journey through grief to a better place.

The reader also needs to know something about my background and the relevant experience I bring to the conversation. My chief qualification is I have personally experienced profound grief in the unexpected death of my wife. In addition, as a minister, I have traveled the journey of grief with several hundred families as they faced their own "valley of the shadow of death." I am familiar with grief and its many manifestations.

This book is written for the person experiencing grief. This is not a book for grief researchers or mental health professionals. I want to provide the nonspecialist with insights to make their journey through grief a bit more tolerable. I am suggesting to all parties involved that it's well past time to come up with a more helpful way of thinking about grief—tsunami is one.

Let me also offer a word about the limits of this book. In the book, I am focused primarily on the death of immediate family members and the grief that comes with those deaths. Insights about grief can easily be extended to other arenas: the death of pets, the loss of jobs, declining health, financial reversals, the loss of friendships, and a host of similar transitions in life. While each of these transitions and heartaches is worthy of a chapter or more in a book, all are beyond the scope of this one.

I encourage you to embrace information or insights in this book that may be helpful; disregard the rest.

Chapter 1

The Tsunami Image

I settled on the tsunami image after a rather lengthy intellectual struggle with my own grief. I found the metaphors and images of grief in every nook and cranny of the internet to be confusing and genuinely unhelpful. In this chapter, I present tsunami as a better proposal.

An image related to water is as natural as anything in the world. In appealing to a water image, I am attempting to place grief in the larger context of the natural world. Birth and the natural celebration of life that comes with it is as normal and everyday as death and the grief that comes with it. Grief is not an oddity. It is not unusual or unnatural. Death and the grief that comes with it are part of the cycle of life and are as routine as the cycle of nature: spring, summer, fall, and winter.

Settling on a natural world context for grief offers a few insights.

There is nothing surprising, bizarre, or life-shattering about death and grief. For thousands of years, creatures on Earth have moved through the natural cycle of life and death. We homo sapiens developed elaborate burial rituals and perspectives on death and grief. In much of our evolutionary history, death was viewed as a natural end to life. With the tsunami image, I am deliberately refocusing the conversation about death and grief to the larger context of the natural world.

I watched a squirrel die the other day; it didn't happen all at once but over a few hours. I live on a four-acre isolated lot, mostly of hardwood trees. Besides the footprint of the house and a small patch of grass, everything else is devoted to trees. It seems we have a bumper crop of squirrels this year. While moving about with yardwork, I noticed a squirrel lying upright on its tummy with all four feet on the ground. As my walking direction was to take me within ten feet of the squirrel, I fully expected it to scamper away and up a nearby white oak tree. Instead, the squirrel hopped a few times and resumed his position. I returned in that direction about fifteen minutes later, but the squirrel had not moved. I stopped and watched the squirrel. Having been alerted by my footsteps, the squirrel opened its eyes. As I stood motion-less, the squirrel's eyes closed slowly. The way the squirrel's eyes closed reminded me of my rare mid-afternoon nap. Sometimes, after a poor night's sleep and a brisk morning of activity in the yard, I find my eyelids getting heavy mid-afternoon while I am sitting on the couch reading. The urge to give in to heavy eyelids can be irresistible. I watched the squirrel for a moment more and then quietly went on about my yard work.

Thirty minutes later, I purposely walked back to check on the squirrel. His chin rested gently on top of his front feet, and he was stretched out, still balanced on all four feet. I got within five feet of the squirrel before it even struggled to open its eyes—barely.

Almost an hour later, I returned to check on the squirrel. On this visit, I wore gloves that extended over my wrists. I slowly walked over to the squirrel. The squirrel did not react. I slipped my right hand under the squirrel's chest. The squirrel reacted with a struggling effort to move its back legs but never opened its eyes. I slipped my left hand under the squirrel's hindquarter, supporting its back legs, and the movement and struggle stopped. I carried the squirrel to an isolated part of the lot where a tree had fallen; the small root ball provided some protection, and I placed the squirrel in the cavity next to the root ball. I surmised I was allowing the squirrel to die in peace in a safer, less exposed place.

The next day, I checked on the squirrel. It was gone. Apparently, a creature of the night assisted the cycle of nature. Death is as natural as birth.

We tend to complicate death. Virtually all funeral services and traditions are for the living, not the deceased. When I officiate at a funeral, I do so within the framework of the Christian tradition. I present a Christian perspective on death and dying. I encourage, support, and help those who grieve by reminding them of the values and tenets of our shared and familiar worldview. In the funeral service, I do what clergy of every faith community do: remind people of the faith community's values and encourage those who grieve to do so in ways consistent with that particular faith tradition.

The values and tenets of many faith communities waft through American culture, creating a complex blend of aromas like a botanical garden in blooming season. In the American amalgamation of ideas, individual faith traditions articulate their perspectives on death and dying more strongly to secure their market share. Then, there are brainstorming entrepreneurs who write books and design webpages to make a few dollars off the swirling confusion about death, dying, and grieving in the marketplace.

The bouquet gets more complex. Modern psychology turns its attention to death, dying, and grieving. Research is conducted, books are written, and training workshops are provided. Psychologists inject their values and tenets into the larger conversation. Neuroscientists have entered the conversation in recent years with their brain scans, values, and tenets.

The complexity created around death and grief by faith communities, psychologists, and neuroscientists pale in comparison to the convoluted complexity produced by special interests in American culture. As a small example, consider health and beauty interests. In the United States, everyone generally wants to look younger if possible. According to statista.com, the United States in 2021 led the world with 5,355,604 nonsurgical cosmetic procedures and 1,992,296 surgical procedures (7,347,900 total).[1] The next closest country was Brazil, with 1,089,420 and 1,634,220, respectively (2,723,640 total). In the case of the United States in 2021, 3.4 percent of adults ages twenty-five to seventy-five underwent some cosmetic procedure that year.[2]

These numbers include surgical repairs from accidents and surgery related to quality-of-life issues. The numbers illustrate that Americans seem obsessed with all things young and beautiful. This obsession has significantly complicated the experience of grief. In a culture that idolizes youth, vitality, and vigor and defines beauty exclusively with traits of the young, it is hard to have a natural and healthy view of aging, let alone death or grief. Those focused on 'young and beautiful' tend to see aging, physical decline, and death as an aberration or abnormality. In their twisted logic, there is something "unnatural" in death, something that causes us to turn away.

In summer 1989, I was out of the office seeing hospitalized congregational members. I was in the neighborhood

---

1. Gianluca Campiglio, ed. *ISAPS International Survey on Aesthetic/Cosmetic Procedures Performed in 2021* (Mount Royal, NJ: ISAPS [International Society of Aesthetic Plastic Surgery], 2022), 15. Available at https://www.isaps.org/media/vdpdanke/isaps-global-survey_2021.pdf.

2. Ibid., 15–16.

and stopped by an assisted living facility; I heard earlier that a church member, Al, was near the end of his earthly journey.

When I walked into his room, I noticed his wife, daughter, and son were huddled around his bed. Walking closer to the bed, I heard the labored breathing that characterizes life's last hours. I had not realized before that moment I would be walking into a family vigil waiting for the death of a loved one. Once there, I did everything we pastors are trained to do in those situations. I had been there maybe seven minutes, and there wasn't a noticeable change in Al's breathing, though it was significantly labored. It was apparent his breathing pattern would not last for hours longer. I thought it might be a good time for me to slip out and leave the family to their dutiful vigil.

Then suddenly, the wife said, "I don't think I can watch this any longer. I am going to go home." The daughter immediately said, "I know this is hard for you, Mom. Come on, let me get you home." The daughter nodded toward her brother and said, "Sam, you stay until Dad dies. Then, call us and let us know." With that, she and her mother turned and left the room.

My thoughts about slipping out changed a bit. I looked at the son to see how he was handling things. Al's breathing was beginning to change; his breathing was slower. After about five minutes, I was again wondering about leaving but was conflicted about leaving the son alone. Then, the son turned to me and said, "I can't watch this either. Pastor, will you stay here with Dad until he dies and then call me and let me know?"

I stayed with Al until he breathed his last. I alerted the nurse through the call system on the bed. She and a co-worker came immediately to confirm Al was not breathing and there was no pulse. One of the nurses left the room to contact a doctor about making the death official.

I then called the son. He wanted to know what his father's last moments were like. I provided as much detail as possible. Sam called his sister and told her of their father's passing. The son related the details I shared with him. I am sure Sam never offered information about his inability to stay for the duration; I never mentioned it either. I don't fault family members for not staying the distance. I was glad to provide "cover" for the son; nothing good would have come from revealing that I alone witnessed Al's death. I would also add that this wasn't the first time, nor last, this kind of thing happened to me. In American culture, we are uncomfortable with everything associated with death. Al's family members were more focused on avoiding death than the familial duty to hold the hand of the one dying. This was not unique to Al's family. It is reflective of American culture.

In the face of all this complexity, the squirrel dying in my yard adds a striking note of simplicity. In the tsunami image, I invite a conversation about death and grief rooted in the natural world. Death and grief have been an integral part of the human condition and experience for tens of thousands of years, long before scientific research, American special interests, and the major faith communities of our world.

I propose we root the conversation about death and grief in the natural world and allow all insights from special interests and faith communities into it, as they help us gain a fuller and more complete sense of death and grief. These non-natural world perspectives have insights to share, and those perspectives have been the subjects of books on grief in the past; for the reader interested in a niche perspective on grief, ample resources are available.

Tsunami invites us to see death, dying, and grief in the helpful context of the natural world. Death happens. It comes to the young and old. It comes as a shocking surprise and as a welcomed friend at the end of a long struggle. Viewing death from the context of the natural world and natural processes minimizes much of the emotional drama and intellectual gymnastics so often associated with death in the modern world.

In American culture, we tend to handle the death of persons of advanced age (in their nineties or one hundred or more) well. The slow decline associated with advanced age helps prepare the audience. With sudden deaths of people more in the prime of physical life or the deaths of children, teenagers, and young adults, we tend to think of death as unnatural. The unrecognized truth is these deaths are normal as well.

After the sudden death of my wife, I began paying more attention to the frequency of similar deaths. It happens much more than most of us realize. The deaths we identify as unusual from our "young and beautiful" perspective are regular and routine; they happen all the time. We tend to recognize them as unusual because they contradict our cultural perspective.

When we are in the throes of severe grief, we are not attempting to dissect our experience into genuine loss as opposed to the disorientation that comes when our cultural framework is upended. In the days after a significant death, we feel overwhelmed: thoughts and feelings are all jumbled together. Having lived for a season in Florida, an adage comes to mind: "When you are fighting alligators, it is hard to remember the mission to drain the swamp."

This is an appropriate place to acknowledge one of the sub-themes of this book, which is to think analytically about the experience of grief. To be sure, most of what we experience in the loss of a loved one is pure and simple grief: we are saddened at the passing of a loved one. In addition to straightforward grief, the death of a loved one can trigger a reevaluation of one's worldview; that is, it can cause a crisis of faith or turn a cultural perspective on its head.

In other chapters of this book, I will return to this subject. Obviously, I am not suggesting an analytical approach for the person caught in the deep struggle of grief. Rather, I am convinced this new perspective on grief can be helpful to those beyond the initial crisis who want to better understand their experience. I am also suggesting that if we can raise people's consciousness prior to a severe experience of grief, we can help prepare them for the challenge ahead.

The varied intensities associated with tsunamis translate well into the arena of grief. Tsunamis may be modest or extreme. This mirrors the actual experience of grief. The weight and intensity of grief vary widely, even among those closest to the deceased.

I remember stopping to see if a mechanic had time to change the oil in my car and ended up becoming a prospective officiant at a funeral. I stopped at the Exxon station just down the street from the church where I served as senior pastor. There wasn't an open timeslot, so I was not able to get my oil changed. I learned that one of the mechanics, Bill, had died, and the family was looking for someone to officiate at the funeral service.

So, I was asked, "You don't know any preachers, do you?" After a brief conversation, I left my name and cell phone number.

An hour later, I had an interesting conversation with Bill's daughter. After introducing herself, she said, "So, I hear you are a preacher."

I acknowledged the fact I was a pastor and expressed sympathy for her loss.

"Are you, like, a real preacher? Do you have a church?" she asked.

I noted that I was a pastor, and the church I served was just a few blocks down the street from the Exxon station where Bill worked. She struggled a bit to pinpoint the church's location until I mentioned that it was "across the street from Starbucks." She immediately knew its exact location. After a few more minutes on the phone, she invited me to Bill's home later in the evening to talk about some of the details of the funeral service.

I arrived close to 6:30 p.m. Apparently, family and friends had gathered at the home for a meal, and I was arriving at the end of the meal. I remember the small house was really crowded. I also remember I was treated as royalty—I think everyone was relieved a "real preacher" had agreed to officiate at the funeral.

I sat in a chair in the living room as friends and family just kept streaming into the already crowded room. The daughter I had spoken to on the phone introduced me to immediate family members. We dialogued for a few minutes about the specifics of the funeral service. Then, I acknowledged I did not know Bill and asked the assembled group to "tell me about Bill." After initial hesitancy, the stories began cascading out. Apparently, Bill was quite the "ringer." Over the next fifteen minutes, I became an observer as the room was taken over by one person after another, telling stories about Bill. Many of the stories were hilarious and included language not appropriate for a funeral eulogy. While the room was taken over by funny stories, not everyone was laughing. Based on body language and facial expressions, some family members were struggling with the kind of sadness that makes laughter artificial.

That crowded living room was an exaggerated manifestation of what I have seen hundreds of times over the years. People deal with grief differently. There are no common threads uniting everyone's expression of grief. Some family members tell funny stories as a way of dealing with their grief. Others experience a sadness akin to mild depression.

These different responses might well come from two people equally close to the deceased.

The tsunami image provides for varied intensities to be experienced by individuals resulting from the same death. This may feel a little counterintuitive as most of us have seen videos of tsunamis coming ashore as a long, massive wave of generally the same height up and down the beach. I acknowledge that a single tsunami wave tends to equally impact everyone on the same beach. And I hope my readers will recognize that any image of grief has its limits. There is no exact and perfect image embodying the experience of grief.

I think the tsunami image is still helpful in that it allows for various intensities of grief. To press my point a bit, there are examples of tsunamis that impact at significantly different intensities.

The Lituya Bay (Alaska) landslide of 1958 generated a tsunami exceeding seventeen hundred feet in height. Lituya Bay is one hundred miles north and west of Juneau, Alaska, on the coast. The bay is basically a rectangular-shaped body of water fed by glaciers to the east. On the northern side of the eastern edge of the bay is Gilbert Inlet; the inlet stretches for about a mile north. In 1958, a landslide occurred on the eastern side of Gilbert Inlet, generating a massive wall of water that slammed into the western side of the inlet at a height of 1,720 feet. As Lituya Bay is slightly south and west of the direct hit area of the tsunami, it experienced smaller wave heights from five hundred feet to around two hundred feet.[3]

The Lituya Bay tsunami is an example of a tsunami with varying wave heights depending on proximity to the original landslide.

---

3. Don J. Miller, *Giant Waves in Lituya Bay Alaska; Geological Survey Professional Paper 354-C* (Washington: US GPO, 1960). Available at https://pubs.usgs.gov/pp/0354c/report.pdf.

There are other examples of tsunamis. The asteroid that created the Chicxulub crater in the Yucatan Peninsula sixty-five million years ago created a tsunami wave of over three hundred feet. It crashed into relatively shallow water. Had it crashed into a deep part of the ocean it's wave would have been measured in miles of height. Many readers will remember the forty-six-foot-high tsunami wave that hit Fukushima, Japan in March 2011; it was caused by an earthquake.

Tsunami provides a common-sense way to think about recovery. If the tsunami wave is measured in inches, it will be barely noticeable. A tsunami of several feet might draw a curious crowd to the beach to observe it making landfall. With a mega-tsunami no one rushes down to the beach to watch it come in—at least none who survives to tell about it. A tsunami of inches will tend to work itself out over time. Nature will take its course, and few will be different for the experience. A tsunami measured in increments of ten feet is another matter entirely. These will result in major devastation, and we can imagine those who get through those events will need some help along the way.

A twenty-foot-high tsunami comes ashore. Those homes facing the beach are largely destroyed, maybe washed off foundations. Homes in low-lying geographical areas, even far from the beach, will experience significant water and flood damage. Homes on higher ground may experience modest damage. It is the same tsunami, but the experience of individual homeowners is very different. In that kind of situation, homeowners are always surprised: they live far from the beach but do not realize they are so close to a floodplain.

The image of grief as a tsunami includes the sense that individuals will recover in the aftermath of loss and grief. Yet, the nature of that recovery/progress is left completely unidentified, and rightly so, as each person's experience of tsunami/grief will be unique.

The life cycle of tsunamis provides a helpful way of thinking about grief. In the case of tsunamis, there is an event that creates them—a landslide or an earthquake. As a result of the event, waves rise and wash ashore. Then, just as naturally, the waves subside, and life returns to more normal levels. Granted, in the wake of a tsunami, there is a lot to clean up—a lot of devastation and a lot of inconvenience.

I am suggesting the pattern of a tsunami (event, a rush of water, an overwhelming experience followed by receding water that eventually returns to something like normal) may mirror the life cycle of grief.

Significant tsunamis forever change the landscape. This, too, provides a helpful way of thinking about moving forward with grief. Instead of imagining that grief will be over at some point, the tsunami image clearly establishes the sense that recovery is a lengthy process and will, inevitably, mean that the future has forever been changed by the significant natural event.

Hurricane Camille made landfall east of New Orleans in August 1969 and marched north through Mississippi and eastern Tennessee before taking a right turn through the southern parts of Kentucky and Virginia. The hurricane dropped at least twenty-seven inches of rain in Nelson County, Virginia, in a little more than an hour. The quantity of rainfall in such a short time caused massive rock and mudslides. In effect, the soil on steep mountainsides, accumulated over thousands of years, was literally washed away. If you drive down Interstate 81 today, you can still see exposed slices of mountain sides—scars from 1969.

Tsunamis provide us with a compelling parallel to the experience of grief in terms of human limitations. Most of us will know about ocean waves on the beach (largely an East Coast experience). Most will know about bracing oneself for the incoming wave: feet firmly semi-embedded in the sand, leaning into the incoming wave with an arm and shoulder to reduce one's profile when the wave arrives. Of course, no strategy really works when facing a tsunami. Under the best of circumstances, with a tsunami wave, you hold your breath as the wave lifts you off your feet and takes you where it wills. Significant grief is not so much something we manage as it is something we survive.

I am not suggesting we are powerless in the face of severe or profound grief; I am suggesting most of what we find in modern American culture is overly optimistic about the individual's ability to manage grief. I am convinced we will do much better if we begin with the premise that grief, especially significant grief, is like a tsunami.

While the tsunami metaphor may seem discouraging, this is a hopeful book. The book suggests we can reclaim a healthy perspective on life. Even so, significant grief forever changes us as individuals; we can never go back to being the person we were before our loss.

Chapter 2

Identifying Myths

Myths are rooted in human psychological fears and can quickly take on a life of their own. Misinformation, rumor, innuendo, distrust, and outright fear seem to be the fertile soil that nurtures myth.

I remember well the Y2K myth. In late fall 1999, some people were convinced all computer systems would come to a crashing halt at 12:00:01 a.m. on January 1, 2000. The myth was that computers were not equipped to deal with the change of a century. I remember two specific conversations around the Y2K craze.

Over coffee one morning, an acquaintance encouraged me to prepare for Y2K by stockpiling canned goods in a basement or spare bedroom. My coffee mate was convinced that on January 1, 2000, all computer systems in the country would crash. He interpreted this to mean all grocery stores would be unable to check people out, so you couldn't pay for groceries. In fact, you would not be able to access your money in the bank because all banking systems would crash as well. In the waning months of 1999, the Y2K myth was alive and well.

I also remember a phone conversation with an elderly woman. I had called to check in and see how she was doing. She immediately began with Y2K and was convinced she would not be able to access her money at the bank after January 1st. I had little success trying to console her. Logic was not an option. Finally, to provide some measure of comfort, I said, "Miss Bessy, if on January 1 all the computers crash and you cannot get any money from your bank, I will come to your apartment and give you three hundred dollars."

"Oh, that would be great," she said. My promise of three hundred dollars apparently calmed her down, and shortly thereafter, we ended the conversation. I debunked one myth with another. The second myth was that I walked around with a wad of one-hundred-dollar bills in my pocket and could just peel off a few whenever I wanted to. Sometimes, you must speak the language people understand.

We love our myths.

I have lived in the Richmond, Virginia, area for thirty-five of the last forty-seven years. I never imagined I would live long enough to see Confederate statues removed from Monument Avenue. The well-established myth was the statues were in honor of Virginia war heroes and had nothing to do with slavery. Then, when the effort to remove the statues began to emerge, the myth morphed into "You can't re-write history" and became the mantra of those who wanted the statues left in place. In the end, we Richmonders learned a lot about history and why the Confederate statues were erected long before any of us were born. While myth can be very resilient, truth can erode the foundations of myth if given enough time.

My twelve-year-old granddaughter was sitting at the school lunchroom table with a few friends one day. She mentioned that she received the Covid shot the previous afternoon. "It didn't hurt very much, either," she said. A classmate responded, "That is terrible. Now you will not be able to have children."

Think of the myths that have been evident in modern American life: Young George Washington "cannot tell a lie"; baseball was invented in Cooperstown; Columbus discovered America; Walt Disney drew Mickey Mouse; cowboys wore cowboy hats; Pocahontas fell in love with John Smith; Thomas Edison invented the electric light bulb; Betsy Ross designed and sewed the first American flag; the Founding Fathers were Christians; the battle of the Alamo was fought to keep America free; the Puritans came to the New World seeking religious freedom; the Liberty Bell cracked on July 4, 1776; the American dream; the myth of equality; the fountain of youth; the self-made man; Seattle is one of the rainiest cities in America; you need to drink eight glasses of water a day; mice love cheese; sugar makes kids hyperactive; left-brained people are logical and right-brained people are creative; playing classical music to babies makes them grow up smarter.

I will stop at this point. I could go on. For a variety of known and unknown reasons, we homo sapiens tend to love our myths. Let me mention a few myths that congregate around grief.

Grief Is Grief

"Grief is grief" is a nonsensical comment often made by people who have never wrestled with deep grief. It is just one of those statements people say to fill the void of silence when they don't know what else to say. "Grief is grief" tends to suggest that grief has a similar path and timeline for all people.

Nothing could be farther from the truth. Grief is as unique as a fingerprint. Everyone needs to follow the pathway that works for them. The myth that we all will experience a similar pathway through grief makes grieving more difficult and complex for those who suffer loss.

In March 2021, a professional acquaintance texted me and asked me to come by my home for a chat. His wife had died several months earlier, and he thought a conversation with me might be helpful. We sat on the front porch of my home. He talked, and I mostly listened. We covered a host of topics and concerns. I specifically remember him saying to me: "Ron, I know that I am supposed to be angry about Millie's death, but I'm not. I don't feel anger at all. I feel grateful for the years we shared. We got to say goodbye to one another. We had a wonderful run for nearly forty years. I don't feel angry. Now, I feel guilty that I am not angry about her death."

Somewhere along his journey, my friend accepted the notion that every person is supposed to feel anger at the death of a loved one. He had tried to feel angry about his wife's death but just couldn't pull it off. Some people do experience anger at the death of a loved one. My friend did not, and I didn't feel anger at the death of my wife.

The notion that the path and timetable of grief will be similar for individuals is not only a myth, but these kinds of myths complicate grief for many. My friend had spent untold emotional energy focused on trying to understand his lack of anger and thinking it might be a sign of some deep trouble in his grief journey. When, in fact, he wrestled with a mirage, a myth.

In his book *Ghosts of the Tsunami*, Richard Lloyd Parry tells the true story of Naomi, the tragedy of the Okawa Elementary School, and the tsunami that hit eastern Japan on March 11, 2011. Residents of Japan are familiar with earthquakes. On the early afternoon of March 11, a Friday, there was a series of tremors and then a significant earthquake. The earthquake and resulting tsunami claimed the lives of 18,500 people and set in motion the nuclear power plant meltdown at the Fukushima Dai-ichi reactor. In the book, Parry offers some insights about grief.

From the survivors of the tsunami, I learned that everyone's grief is different and that it differs in small and subtle ways according to the circumstances of loss. "The first thing was this," said Naomi. "Did you lose your children, or did your children survive? That divided people immediately: the children who lived and those who died." Thirty-four of the 108 pupils at the school survived the wave—because they had been picked up in time by their parents or crawled miraculously out of the water.

Even among the bereaved there were graduations of grief, a spectrum of blackness indiscernible to those on the outside. It came down to a coldhearted question: once the water had retreated, how much did you have left? Sayomi Shito had lost her beloved daughter Chisato; it would have been unthinkably callous to point out that her two older children, her husband, her extended family, and her home were unharmed and intact.

There also was the matter of finding the deceased and burying them . . . some didn't have that luxury.[1]

People have very different experiences with grief.

Moving Past Grief

Of all the things that might be said of grief, "moving past grief" may be the most outrageous. The notion that we will move past grief may make sense at the death of an acquaintance or distant relative. Sure, if the guy who handed me my morning coffee through the drive-thru window at Dunkin dies, I might get used to a new person handing me coffee. In fact, I might like the new Dunkin employee better than the previous one. Even so, casual acquaintances who die do not present us with wrestling matches with grief.

---

1. Richart Lloyd Parry, *Ghosts of the Tsunami: Death and Life in Japan's Disaster Zone* (New York: MCD Books, 2017), 172–73.

When we experience severe or profound grief, there is no moving past it. This becomes obvious in the following questions. If a mother loses a two-year-old child to cancer, do you think that young mother will ever move past that grief? For a couple who shared sixty-five years of marriage and one person dies, do you think the survivor will ever move past grief?

Or more up to date, if a father and daughter are sitting together at a baseball game and an active shooter shows up and begins firing wildly into the crowd, and a bullet hits the daughter before the father can move in front of her to take the bullet—in what universe will the father "move past" his daughter's tragic and senseless death?

We don't move past grief. We learn to live with it.

Five Stages of Grief

"The five stages of grief" is a modern myth. If the concept of the five stages of grief proved helpful to someone along the journey of grief, it is more an accident than anything else. There simply are not five stages to grief. Grief is not that simple.

Talk of the five stages of grief is rooted (poorly) in Elisabeth Kübler-Ross's 1969 publication, *On Death and Dying: What the Dying Have to Teach Doctors, Nurses, Clergy and Their Own Families.* As noted in her testimony before the US Senate Special Committee on Aging (August 7, 1972), Dr. Kübler-Ross had interviewed more than five hundred terminally ill patients and "asked them to share with us what it is like to be dying."[2] Dr. Kübler-Ross interviewed and followed more than five hundred patients from the time of

---

2. Elizabeth Kübler-Ross, *On Death and Dying: What the Dying Have to Teach Doctors, Nurses, Clergy and Their Own Families* (New York: Scribner 1969), 283; "Death with Dignity: Hearings before the Special

their terminal diagnosis until their deaths. Her relationship with these patients initially began in the hospital shortly after they received a terminal diagnosis from their medical doctor.

From extensive and highly personal interviews with dying patients, Dr. Kübler-Ross developed five stages of dying; that is, the five stages terminally ill patients tended to move through after their diagnosis. The five stages she identified were denial (and isolation), anger, bargaining, depression, and acceptance. Knowing this background, it is easy to understand why and how a terminally ill patient might go through the five stages. To illustrate, imagine a hospital patient, Bill, who just received a terminal diagnosis from his doctor.

Bill immediately begins:

"Oh, this cannot be true. I don't feel that bad. I bet the hospital got my records mixed up with another person's medical records. I really don't feel that bad." Virtually every reader can easily imagine how Bill's first reaction might be denial, the first of the five stages.

"Well, damn. This is just terrible. Why am I the one who gets this diagnosis? Why me? I've lived a reasonably good life." We can easily understand that Bill's denial might have morphed into anger. Who would not be angry with a terrible diagnosis?

And who would not expect Bill's bargaining: "Lord, you healed many people in the Bible. How about me? Lord, if you make this illness go away, I will live a better life. I will dedicate myself to a better future." Of course, this brings to mind Scrooge's bargaining with the Angel of Death in *A Christmas Carol.*

When reality began to settle in, who among us could fault Bill for feeling depressed (the fourth stage of the five)?

Committee on Aging," United States Senate, August 7, 1972, https://www.aging.senate.gov/imo/media/doc/publications/871972.pdf.

And at some point, Bill accepts the terminal diagnosis.

The five stages apply easily and naturally to Bill and most of the people we can imagine receiving a terminal diagnosis. They should. Kübler-Ross developed the five stages after interviews with hundreds of people just like Bill.

Dr. Kübler-Ross's book is mostly remembered as the manifesto of the hospice movement. In addition, it is remembered as a critique of the historic authoritarian perspective of modern medicine; Kübler-Ross suggested the patient's values and wishes should be considered in the practice of medicine. There is nothing in her 1969 publication to suggest there are five stages of grief.

How, then, did the five stages of grief become associated with Kübler-Ross?

Following the publication of her book, Kübler-Ross became a bit of a media darling, landing interviews with national news organizations, numerous magazines, and major newspapers. In the wake of her popularity, entrepreneurs began applying the five stages to a countless number of experiences, including grief. "Five stages of grief" stuck in the popular imagination. On numerous occasions, Kübler-Ross had the opportunity to correct the record by simply noting her research was about the stages dying patients experienced, not stages of grief, but she declined to make those corrections. Thus, she fueled the misconceptions of the five stages being applied to grief.

To state what must surely be obvious, there were never clinical studies to support the five stages of grief. In her last book (published after her death), co-authored with David Kessler and titled *On Grief and Grieving: Finding the Meaning of Grief through the Five Stages of Loss*, she confirmed in writing what she had suggested in person for several decades: the five stages apply to grief. Even so, the book reveals an unease with the five stages being applied to grief. Early in the book they write,

> The stages have evolved since their introduction, and they have been very misunderstood over the past three decades. They were never meant to help tuck messy emotions into neat packages. They are responses to loss that many people have, but there is not a typical response to loss, as there is no typical loss. Our grief is as individual as our lives.[3]

It must also be noted that the book's effort to apply the five stages of grief required a lot of verbal gymnastics. In the section on denial, the authors wrote:

> Denial in grief has been misinterpreted over the years. When the stage of denial was first introduced in *On Death and Dying*, it focused on the person who was dying. In this book, *On Grief and Grieving*, the person who may be in denial is grieving the loss of a loved one. In a person who is dying, denial may look like disbelief. They may be going about life and actually denying that a terminal illness exists. For a person who has lost a loved one, however, the denial is more symbolic than literal.[4]

The careful reader must ask, "So, just what is symbolic denial?"

Clearly, for Kübler-Ross, the application of the five stages to grief was never an easy or natural fit.

If there are not five stages of grief, then why did the five stages stick so thoroughly in modern consciousness?

---

3. Elizabeth Kübler-Ross and David Kessler, *On Grief and Grieving: Finding the Meaning of Grief through the Five Stages of Loss* (New York: Scribner, 2004), 7.

4. Ibid., 8.

Some of us are old enough to remember the late 1960s and early 1970s. As the Vietnam War began to wind down, and given all the upheaval of the 1960s, the cultural context in America was filled with uncertainty, ambiguity, and complexity. The five stages offered something concrete, limited, and navigable. Kübler-Ross's research seemed to tame grief and present it in a way that could be managed. People embraced the stages because they offered a pathway through one of life's painful rites of passage.

She also offered the five stages in a season when Americans were eager to embrace clinical studies of all types as proof of a recommended pathway forward. Clinical studies and diagnostic equipment began changing treatment options for cancer in the 1970s. At the same time, sonography, CT scans, and PET scans created better and more precise ways to understand diseases and the physical realities of the human body. It was a season for believing in what medical science was bringing to our doorsteps.

We now know there was "soft research" behind Kübler-Ross's five stages of dying; her research did not meet the standards associated with clinical trials in our country today. We also know there was no research on applying the five stages to grief.

Five stages of grief is a modern myth created in the years after the publishing of the Kübler-Ross book of 1969.

In addition, the five stages do not fit the actual experience of grief. Over the years, people have used the five stages and books written about them as resources to help them through grief. If the five stages help someone with their grief, then we all are delighted. If the five stages help in one person's grief journey or in the journeys of 100,000 people, it still does not prove there are five stages to grief. It simply affirms a book about stages of grief was helpful. There are many practical concerns with the concept of the five stages of grief.

At some point in the book, I wanted to relate my own experience with grief. Here is probably a good place to start.

On March 21, 2016, I returned home after a dinner meeting to find my wife of forty-two years dead on the floor beside the kitchen table, face down. My wife died earlier in the day from a completely unexpected massive heart attack. Based on the coroner's report, she would have died even if the heart attack had occurred in an emergency room.

On finding my wife, I called 911. I was in a state of shock. As I realized the reality of the situation, I struggled with a strange kind of mental fog. The 911 operator began walking me through several questions: Where is she? Is she breathing? Does she have a pulse? I followed instructions as best I could. I rolled my wife over on her side. Then I realized I didn't need a rescue square or an EMT; I needed a coroner.

Suffice it to say, it was obvious my wife had been dead for a handful of hours.

"Mr. Crawford, are you sure you don't need an ambulance?" the dispatcher asked.

I replied, "I don't need an ambulance. I need a coroner. My wife has been dead for hours."

Shortly, a deputy arrived at my door and asked hastily, "Where is your wife?" I pointed to the kitchen area, and he hustled into the room. He was immediately on the phone confirming my wife was dead and there was no need for an EMT.

A second police car arrived and then began the due diligence process associated with deaths like my wife's: "Mr. Crawford, when did you arrive home? Where had you been? When did you leave? Are there people who can confirm your absence from the home?" If you have had this kind of experience, you know you get asked the same series of questions over and over by different officials.

I called and asked a friend to come by. I knew Joe, a local minister, would be helpful as I needed to make phone calls to my adult children, and I doubted I would be able to tell them their mother was dead. A colleague, Melissa, showed up and sat with me.

The coroner arrived and began processing her body to be transported.

I sat in the living room with two dear friends. It is funny what you say in those moments. I told both my friends, "You cannot go in the kitchen and see my wife." My wife was always concerned about the way she looked, and she would have never wanted to be viewed lying on the floor dead. It seems even amid significant mental fog; I was determined to protect her privacy.

Let's see how my experience may or may not have aligned with the five stages of grief. Denial is the first stage identified in the five stages.

To say it bluntly, what is there to deny when your wife is lying on the floor dead in the next room? Denial was never part of my experience. Granted, if someone tells you your loved one has died, you may have questions until you see the body. Once you have seen the body, there is no denial.

I experienced no anger at any time, not the evening when I found my wife, and not since. From the first moment, my deepest and most profound concern was for my children and grandchildren. I didn't have the luxury to feel anger, to act as if my wife's death was really all about me. I suspect my reaction was close to the average or normal reaction to sudden, unexpected deaths.

The third stage of the five stages is bargaining. So, how do you bargain when your wife lies cold and dead on the floor? One may bargain with a terminal diagnosis. There is no bargaining with death. My wife was dead when I found her.

And to jump ahead, acceptance of my wife's death is what sent me into a mental fog within seconds of finding her. I never had an option to not accept my wife's death.

Maybe a year-and-a-half after my wife's death, a friend's wife died nine weeks after a cancer diagnosis. The surviving husband said, "I never felt any anger at all with Susan's death. Quite the contrary, I felt nothing but gratitude for the wonderful years we shared together. I got every caring husband's dream: I held my wife as she slipped into the other world."

To add validity to the case I am making, let me describe another person's experience.

My cousin Mary had a different experience with the death of her husband. Charles was feeling bad and ended up going to the doctor. The doctor prescribed an antibiotic. In a week, Charles was back with more symptoms; things were getting worse, not better. After a few days of tests, the specialist provided the diagnosis—stage four cancer.

Charles and Mary fought against cancer in one of the most heroic battles ever recorded. Even so, there came the decision to call in hospice. Six weeks later, Charles died in his home with his family at his side.

How do the five stages apply to Mary's grief? She never experienced denial. She knew something was wrong when Charles went to the doctor for the first time. She became more concerned when he didn't get better with the antibiotic. She was half expecting a bad report from the specialist as she had seen Charles's decline. Mary was with her husband almost constantly. She was a witness to his declining health. There was no denying what she saw and experienced.

Once the diagnosis came, Mary had no time for anger, bargaining, depression, acceptance, or denial; with every ounce of her being, she supported her husband's fight against cancer. When the decision came to call in hospice, she only felt admiration and love for her husband. With deep satisfaction and love, she remembers Charles's final moments with his children.

There were no five stages to grief for Mary or her adult children. I didn't experience any of the so-called five stages of grief, nor did my friend with the death of his wife, Susan. As I noted in the introduction, I have walked with several hundred families through the death of a family member. I am hard-pressed to identify any of those families who experienced five stages of their grief. And maybe more importantly, I can remember many of those families questioning their experience of grief because it did not match common expectations about grief in American culture.

The five stages must be abandoned if we want to provide help to those among us who are grieving.

Chapter 3

What Is Profound Grief?

The local obituary read:

Local businessman Gregarious Greg, age seventy-one, died on Sunday evening after a brief illness. Gregarious Greg will be sorely missed by his family and the many patrons with whom he has developed friendships over the years. His funeral will be on Thursday at 2 p.m. at Metcalf's Funeral Home. He is survived by his three children: Logical Logan, Sentimental Sam, and Estranged Edna.

In the imaginary obituary above, we can begin to decipher how grief might affect those connected to Gregarious Greg.

Obviously, patrons will miss seeing and chatting with Gregarious Greg. We might say of them, "They will miss Gregarious Greg, but his death does not rise to the level of grief for them." I define grief for our purposes as persistent sadness, emotional anxiety, and mental fatigue resulting from the death of a person. Some of those patrons may experience a need to attend the funeral "to say goodbye," but most will not. Few, if any, patrons will describe their experience of this death as grief.

On the other hand, Sentimental Sam will experience grief. While certainly a son, Sentimental Sam was never close to his dad. It seems Gregarious Greg was always busy at work or with civic groups and missed a good bit of Sentimental Sam's childhood. Gregarious Greg never quite understood Sentimental Sam's emotional and sentimental side.

After graduating from college, Sentimental Sam moved to a neighboring town some eighty miles from his father and old hometown. Over the years, Sentimental Sam developed his own professional life and friends who understood and appreciated his emotional, warm, and affirming personality. In some ways, Sentimental Sam appreciated all his father did for him but never felt his father really understood or appreciated him. It was most likely this desire to be appreciated and understood that kept Sentimental Sam returning regularly to visit. Of course, Gregarious Greg never spent much time with his son on these visits and was clearly not open to revisiting their adult relationship. Even so, Sentimental Sam kept returning; hope springs eternal.

Sentimental Sam will grieve his father's passing; after all, you only get one dad. Sentimental Sam's grief will likely center on his own emotional disposition and on the lack of resolution in his son-father relationship. His dad is now gone, and the chance to resolve these issues has been forever removed. Sentimental Sam's "unfinished business" will push his grief much deeper than one might expect.

Logical Logan is another matter altogether. Logical Logan was the son who embraced his father's profession as he had worked in the family business since his graduation from high school. In fact, Logical Logan had at times argued with his father about the direction of the family business. On several occasions, Gregarious Greg said to his son, "I am running the business now. When I am dead and gone, you, Logical Logan, will be able to run it any way you want. But for now, we do things my way." Logical Logan tends to view his father's death from an entirely different perspective from that of Sentimental Sam. Logical Logan knows that death is as natural as birth; after all, we all die. His father's death was going to happen sooner or later. The fact it happened sooner means that Logical Logan will be able to run the family business sooner. Sure, he will miss his dad, but life goes on.

It is clear Logical Logan's grief will be modest: he doesn't have a sentimental bone in his body, and he has actually been waiting for his father to pass. At some point in the future as he gets more deeply into his responsibilities running the family business, he may develop a deeper appreciation for his father. Even then, it will be an appreciation of his father—not necessarily grief.

In the case of Estranged Edna, she may feel a sense of relief at her father's passing. After all, she developed a negative view of her dad long ago. When her mother divorced her father, Estranged Edna sided with her mother. In the intervening decades, she has consistently distanced herself from her father. One wonders if she will experience any grief at all. She might well respond to news of his death with, "Oh, I guess that means I am expected to attend his funeral."

With Sentimental Sam, I noted he had "unfinished business" with his father. We don't get the sense that Estranged Edna has "unfinished business" with her father. From her side of the equation, it seems she is happy with the relationship she had with her father at the time of his death. With Estranged Edna, there is a small chance she will experience grief sometime after the funeral in terms of wishing she had said a few more things to her dad while he was alive. Even so, we don't get the sense that Estranged Edna has lingering issues that might come back to bite her weeks after the funeral. She seems pretty settled in terms of her relationship with her dad. Her solid relationship with her mother also seems to argue against a somewhat delayed experience of grief.

What is clearly apparent is that Gregarious Greg's three children will have very different experiences of grief.

There are a few others in the picture but not mentioned in the obituary. Distant Diane was once married to Gregarious

Greg. They divorced when the children were teenagers. Distant Diane's major complaint was Gregarious Greg was never home; she threw in the towel with Gregarious Greg's third affair—the third one she knew about. In subsequent decades, Distant Diane finished her teaching degree and ended up in the local middle school as a math teacher. In fact, most of the community never knew or had forgotten that she once was married to Gregarious Greg. While past the age of normal retirement, Distant Diane continued to enjoy her job and is building up retirement benefits as she finished her degree in her mid-forties and for years was a stay-at-home mom. Of the children, to no one's surprise, she kept up closely with Estranged Edna and Sentimental Sam but rarely saw Logical Logan. Distant Diane's grief will probably end up being "non-grief." It has been a lot of years, and she has clearly moved past Gregarious Greg's antics.

Then, not known in the larger community is Hopeful Harriet. Gregarious Greg and Hopeful Harriet had been an item for eighteen months. She is thirty-four years old and has no children or family. She admired Gregarious Greg from the moment they first met. Their love was easy, natural, and exciting. Six months into their relationship, Gregarious Greg helped her get a newer and better apartment; his agreement to pay for half the monthly rent made the new apartment possible. Hopeful Harriet was very optimistic about their relationship: she expected to get an engagement ring any day and was thinking they would buy a small house just outside of town. Maybe in time, she would be able to quit her job and be a stay-at-home spouse, maybe in time, a mom. For his part, Gregarious Greg was slowing down a bit given his age, seventy-one, so he seemed well-content with one romantic flame. And truth be told, Hopeful Harriet was excited enough for both.

In Gregarious Greg's death, Hopeful Harriet is going to have a troublesome time. Not only is she losing a lover, a prospective husband and father, but a provider. There is no way she is going to be able to keep the apartment and there is no way she will ever be a stay-at-home-spouse. All her hopes came to a crashing end with Gregarious Greg's death.

Hopeful Harriet will experience profound grief.

Now, let's begin to articulate several important definitions considering the imaginary story above.

As I have already defined, grief is persistent sadness, emotional anxiety, and mental fatigue resulting from the death of a person.

Severe grief might be defined as persistent great sadness, deep emotional anxiety, and near-overwhelming mental fatigue resulting from a person's death.

Profound grief is persistent great sadness, deep emotional anxiety, and overwhelming mental fatigue resulting from a person's death that all force an individual to change their worldview or sense of identity. Profound grief is severe grief with a mental health dimension.

Some will push back on my definition of profound grief and suggest it is two things, not one; two things in that it is severe grief and a separate issue about mental health. I respond by saying that in the case of Hopeful Harriet and many people who experience profound grief, the two are interwoven and cannot be separated, nor should they. For those who experience profound grief, the two are one.

Non-grief is a sense of loss in a person's death, which simply does not rise to the level of grief. People who experience non-grief at someone's death will experience loss, disappointment, and inconvenience. In the case of Gregarious Greg's death, 95 percent or more of those touched by his death will experience what might be called non-grief.

Grief is a normal, natural response to loss. It almost always simply works itself out over months or maybe a few years. For those who experience normal grief, there are really no stages, no levels, and few adjustments that need to be made in day-to-day life because of the death of someone. In the case of Gregarious Greg, most family members will experience grief, more or less: Logical Logan, Estranged Edna, Distant Diane.

Severe grief elicits a deeper and more disconcerting reaction to someone's death. Sentimental Sam will certainly fall into this category. Because of his tender heart and unfinished business with his father, Sentimental Sam will experience grief that may evolve into severe grief. His grief is not apt to tumble into profound grief because he has an established community of friends who provided healthy emotional support, affirming and appreciating his wonderful, warm, caring presence.

Hopeful Harriet's world was completely turned upside down in Gregarious Greg's death. Her world was dramatically changed. Her life course was altered significantly because of Gregarious Greg's death. In the wake of her lover's death, she will experience profound grief.

As I have laid out my definitions for non-grief, grief, severe grief, and profound grief, it may be helpful to contrast my views with those of others.

The American Psychological Association defines grief as: "anguish experienced after a significant loss... it often includes physiological distress, separation anxiety, confusion, yearning, obsessive dwelling on the past . . . ."[1] The *Cambridge Dictionary* defines grief as "Very great sadness, especially at

---

1. "Grief," *American Psychological Association*, https://www.apa.org/topics/grief.

the death of someone."[2] The Mayo Clinic defines grief as "a strong, sometimes overwhelming emotion for people . . . they might find themselves feeling numb and removed from daily life, unable to carry on with regular duties while saddled with their sense of loss."[3]

Most of what others identify as grief I define as severe grief. In my mind, it is helpful to offer four categories of grief to give most, if not everyone, a place to land. Defining grief as "anguish," "physiological distress," and "very great sadness" will exclude 98 percent or more of those who attend a typical funeral. My categories tend to offer everyone a place to land in the conversation.

Let me return to the subject of profound grief to discuss its connection with mental health. An example may be helpful.

On one occasion, I was talking with a friend and learned that many years earlier, he had lost a son. Apparently, the ten-year-old boy ran out to retrieve a ball and was hit by a passing car. It was a terrible accident that created a lot of angst in the local neighborhood. I asked my friend about his grief.

He noted that after his son's death, every Sunday afternoon, he would visit his son's grave.

He said, "I would take a folding lawn chair. I would sit there and talk to my son."

Then he said something that stirred concern on my part, "Yeah, I would sit there, and my son would talk back to me."

"How long did this go on for?" I asked.

"Oh, I guess for a year and a half," he replied.

I asked, "Why did you stop going?"

---

2. "Grief," *Cambridge Dictionary*, https://dictionary.cambridge.org/dictionary/english/grief.

3. "What is grief?" *Mayo Clinic*, https://www.mayoclinic.org/patient-visitor-guide/support-groups/what-is-grief.

"My son stopped talking to me," came the reply.

This very kind of thing happens more often than most people realize. It tends to stem from unresolved issues with the deceased. In the case of my friend, he had a wealth of fatherly advice he wanted to share with his son. His son's premature death robbed this father of the opportunity to share this information with his son. So, every Sunday he went to talk with his son and take care of "unfinished business."

When I learned about my friend's conversations with his son at the grave, my mental health radar lit up like a Christmas tree. This kind of experience may well raise issues about mental health. Even so, thirty years later, when I was having the conversation about his son's death, there were no lingering mental health issues in my friend. He had lived a normal and productive life. His family, with other children, was as happy and well-adjusted as any. Whatever mental health issues, or borderline mental health issues, triggered by his son's death were managed with his trips to the grave.

In his book, *The Other Side of Sadness: What the New Science of Bereavement Tells Us about Life after Loss*, George Bonanno tells the stories of Sondra Beaulieu[4] and Daniel Levy,[5] which are similar to the story I just related about my friend in the preceding paragraphs. In the cases of Sondra and Daniel, they experienced moments when their deceased loved one was "with them." Bonanno, a professor of clinical psychology, also relates in the book, "I have, in fact, periodically engaged in something of a continued relationship with my deceased father."[6] A few paragraphs later, Bonanno writes, "At first, I felt a bit odd speaking out loud. I looked around

---

4. George A. Bonanno, *The Other Side of Sadness: What the New Science of Bereavement Tells Us about Life after Loss* (New York: Basic Books, 2019), 199–203.

5. Ibid., 203–206.

6. Ibid., 206.

to double-check. Nobody was there; nobody was watching me. I spoke at a normal conversational level. 'Hello, Dad.' I began, and then I paused. I didn't hear anything but felt my father's presence. It was warm and comforting."

Many of my readers will know personal mental health is not a fortress on a scale of sanity where we are entrenched and cannot be moved, but rather is like a boat anchored in a bay. Storms can lift the anchor, and we find ourselves moved a bit—sometimes permanently.

Dan McAdams is a professor of psychology and human development. In his book *The Art and Science of Personality Development*, he notes that nature and nurture are central influences making us who we are as individuals. He is innovative in mentioning a third major influence in shaping personality: the role of trauma.[7] My friend noted above was forever changed by the loss of his son.

This makes perfect sense when you think about it. Do you think those who survived Sandy Hook, Columbine, or 9/11 were changed by their experiences?

I mentioned earlier the book *Ghosts of the Tsunami*. It tells the story of Naomi and the death of her daughter. Now may be a good place to share more of that story. In the wake of the earthquake, Naomi wanted to drive down to the valley and pick up her twelve-year-old daughter, Koharu, at the Okawa Elementary School. This wasn't unusual. Typically, parents would pick up their children after an earthquake; it was standard operating procedure. Earthquakes could sometimes cause minor damage at school or on roads, so many parents made a habit of picking up their children on days of an earthquake.

7. Dan P. McAdams, *Stories We Live By: Personal Myths and the Making of the Self* (New York: Morrow, 1993), 293–99; Dan P. McAdams, *The Art and Science of Personality Development* (New York: Guildford, 2015), 218–20.

Unfortunately, this was not a routine earthquake. Electricity and cell phone systems were down, and it was virtually impossible to get information about the extent of damage caused by the earthquake. Naomi decided to wait a bit before she tried to make her way to the school.

At the Okawa Elementary School, administrators followed their earthquake policy, and all children and teachers were quickly escorted out of the building onto nearby athletic fields. As administrators could not access additional information about the earthquake or possible tsunami, they elected to keep everyone together on the athletic field instead of heading up the half mile to higher ground. This proved to be a tragic mistake. When the tsunami wave of water, mud, and debris showed itself, it was too late. The athletic field was flooded in a matter of minutes. The worst was the mud; it tended to trap people—it was impossible to run in mud. In minutes, the mud and water encircled children and their teachers and eventually either washed them away further inland or covered them where they fell.

> In late June, [Naomi] participated in a week-long course at a training center near Sendai. All the other participants were men. They showed no curiosity about Naomi, and she felt no urge to explain herself. At the end of the week, she came away with a license to operate earthmoving equipment, one of the few women in Japan to possess such a qualification. She went immediately to work, borrowing a digger of her own and sifting the mud in search of Koharu.[8]

During the first week of August, Naomi received a text message from the police asking about her daughter Koharu's

---

8. Parry, *Ghosts of the Tsunami*, 75.

clothing on that fateful Friday. It seemed they may have found her body.

Naomi and her husband went to the police station. Naomi asked to see the body. The police chief noted that he didn't think that would be such a good idea as the body was "incomplete."[9]

Naomi, of course, insisted on seeing her daughter's body. What remained of her daughter was a torso without arms, legs, or a head.

There is loss and grief, and then there is this other horrible, terrible experience that is too big, too deep, and too devastating to go by the designation "grief." Stories and experiences like Naomi's led me to the term "profound grief."

As this is an important chapter, let me briefly summarize: I identified several categories in the tsunami of grief: non-grief, grief, severe grief, and profound grief. I have purposely avoided the categories and definitions that others use because I am not writing for the specialist. Most people need categories that make sense to them. They also need to be able to see themselves somewhere on the spectrum of grief.

---

9. Ibid., 119.

Chapter 4

Influencers of Grief

In the world of social media, we have become familiar with the term "influencers." They typically are people with millions of followers who enjoy some measure of influence with those followers. From YouTube celebrities to Instagram sensations, folks in towns nationwide pay attention to influencers.

As it turns out, there may be some significant influencers when it comes to grief.

The Nature of the Shared Relationship

In a previous chapter noting the death of Gregarious Greg, I suggested his children might have significantly different experiences of grief based on the nature of the relationship they shared with their father. I suspect my readers intuitively know this is true.

Several additional examples may be helpful.

I heard through the grapevine that Arjun's father died. I called and left a message on Arjun's cell phone expressing my sympathy. He returned my call and, as I was busy then, left the following message: "Sorry I missed your call. I saw you called but didn't listen to the message, as I was busy with a birthday luncheon for a co-worker. Call me back."

I was a little puzzled by Arjun's message. His father died, yet he was off enjoying a co-worker's birthday luncheon? My mind was put at ease when I finally talked with Arjun. It seems Arjun's birth father died in India; as Arjun was adopted at birth, he never knew his biological father. His father died weeks before, and Arjun's circle of friends were just learning about it. For Arjun, his father's death was an item of interest but not a matter of grief.

I knew Sally was in for a boatload of grief when I heard her mother died. Sally talked on the phone with her mother every day, sometimes two or three times. Somewhat estranged through the high school and college years, the two became close when Sally started her family. Her mother was full of advice and frequently babysat for her grandchildren. Over time, Sally and her mother became best friends as well. Sally shared a unique and deep relationship with her mother. Some would say it was not a typical mother-daughter relationship. Whatever it was, I knew Sally was going to take her mother's death extremely hard.

For most of their marriage, Bill wasn't much of a husband. Saying he had trouble with marital norms would be an understatement. Even so, his wife hung in there with him. A week after their forty-fifth anniversary, Bill had a heart attack. For Bill, the aftermath of the attack became a time of intense re-evaluation. The attack changed his life; he experienced deep remorse for the way he had treated his wife for all those years. He became a man on a mission—to make it up to his wife for all his previous indiscretions. Six months later, she died in an automobile accident at the hands of a drunk driver. Emotionally, Bill crashed—completely crashed. His grief was complex and profound. Four months after his wife's death, Bill died. Some say it was another heart attack. Some say he died of a broken heart riddled with remorse.

Mike and Ray were like peas in a pod; wherever you saw one, the other wasn't far away. When I met them in 2017, they had been together for more than twenty-five years. In addition to being lovers and committed partners, they were best friends. Both were a little quirky; they were the cutest of couples. They married soon after the Supreme Court ruling on October 6, 2014, making gay marriage legal in Virginia. Ray cried like a baby when he learned of Mike's death on the afternoon of November 3, 2022. A friend characterized Ray's grief as a chunk of driftwood battered by waves on the beach. Ray was inconsolable.

I share the above stories (names changed, of course) to illustrate the enormous variety of relationships experienced in the human family and suggest that the nature of the relationship shared with the deceased will directly impact the experience of grief.

Our sense of loss and the degree of grief we experience are related to the depth of the shared relationship.

The Way the Loss Came

How a death arrives matters.

In an earlier chapter, I mentioned the death of my cousin's husband. Mary's husband died in 2014 after a prolonged struggle with cancer. My wife died suddenly eighteen months later in 2016. The following year, we both attended the visitation and funeral service for our last uncle, Joe, in Portsmouth, Virginia. We caught up with each other in the lobby during the visitation for my uncle; the funeral was the next day.

As we talked, Mary began talking about her experience with grief. This is normal for people who have lost a spouse; it is nice to talk with a person who truly understands. As Mary began talking about her grief, I started nodding my head in agreement. A few minutes later, I sensed Mary was anxious and realized I had stopped nodding. I dutifully began nodding my head, and Mary's anxiety subsided. As she was talking about something very private and personal—her grief—she needed me to affirm what she was saying.

I had stopped nodding my head as she described her grief because she was describing aspects of grief I had never experienced. It was a moment of revelation for me. I realized how one's spouse died is a significant influencer of how grief will unfold for the individual.

In Mary's case, her husband died after a long struggle with cancer at home surrounded by family. My wife died alone and unexpectedly—I found her hours after her death. In my wife's death, I was robbed of several precious moments. I didn't have the opportunity to say goodbye. I never had the chance to say what I wanted; I think my last words to her were, "I gotta run, babe," as I hustled out the door headed to a meeting at work. I couldn't comfort her as she stepped over the threshold into a better place.

As Mary described aspects of grief associated with a prolonged illness, I was amazed. She described thoughts and feelings I knew nothing about.

I contrast this with another conversation I had a year earlier. I was back in Asheville visiting friends who had not been able to attend my wife's funeral. I caught up with many of them when I attended the First Baptist Church for a service in August 2016. I had a few meaningful conversations with wonderful old friends. On that occasion, I also talked with a woman whose husband had died suddenly and unexpectedly while hiking. As she spoke of her grief, I found myself nodding eagerly in agreement. Though we were strangers, I could easily have finished her sentences as she talked about her grief. I knew exactly what she was talking about when she talked of her grief. Though we were strangers, we had traveled the same road.

In more recent years, I have encouraged conversations with friends and acquaintances about grief. While twenty-somethings may think conversations about death, dying, and grief odd, those of us in the eighth decade of life find them normal. As I have already noted, I am not a fan of thinking about grief in stages. If grief is to be studied in categories, the place to begin is with the way the spouse died. From my experience, there are significant similarities in grief processes among people based on the circumstances of a spouse's death.

The Role of Culture and Sub-culture

I still remember Wilmer's funeral. I was twenty-six and served as an associate minister of the Montrose Baptist Church on the east side of Richmond, Virginia. The church's senior minister was out of town and unable to get back for the funeral. Consequently, I stepped in to officiate at the funeral. I believe it was the third funeral I had ever conducted.

I was comfortable officiating the funeral as I knew Wilmer and Mazzie well. They lived across the street from the church on Carlisle Avenue. Wilmer was not in good health, but Mazzie attended every Sunday.

The family visitation at the funeral home the night before the funeral went well. On the day of the funeral, I arrived thirty minutes before the funeral. The funeral director noted the casket was open for people to pay their respects before the service. As was the pattern of that funeral home (and community), the casket was open as people gathered for the funeral. Then, just before the service started, a curtain was drawn between the casket and the audience. The family was invited to come by the casket and view the body one more time before the casket was closed and the funeral began.

Mazzie was the last to view the body. She remained by the casket while all other family members returned to their assigned pews. Sitting near the lectern, I noticed the funeral director was having trouble getting Mazzie away from the casket and back to her seat. Mazzie started to cry, then sobbed. It wasn't long before she was wailing loudly. The funeral director was struggling to get Mazzie back to her pew. Then, very surprising to me, Mazzie, wailing and screaming, tried to crawl up into the casket with Wilmer's body. Modesty out the door, she had one leg on the floor and one leg on the casket, trying to climb in with her husband. That is when the funeral director turned to me and said, "You have got to do something."

My first thought was to find Mazzie a stepping stool to help her accomplish the task. All sense of decorum was out the window as I leaned into Mazzie and pried her hand off Wilmer's arm. Getting both her feet back on the floor took me a while. Then, surprisingly, she turned and dutifully walked to her designated pew.

A few days later, I dropped by Mazzie's home to see how she was doing. In that conversation, I learned that Mazzie grew up among what she called "wailing Baptists" in the deep mountains of Appalachia. Her behavior at the funeral was in keeping with the best traditions of "wailing Baptists" in the community where she grew up—not so much for Richmond, Virginia.

Different geographical areas have different traditions around funerals. I remember a traditional wake in a rural community west of Danville, Virginia. Traditional wakes were nearly a thing of the past in 1981 in that community. Yet, with the death of a ninety-six-year-old patriarch, the family decided on a traditional wake. The visitation happened at the family homeplace, a grand, two-story farmhouse. Early in the day, the funeral home delivered the body into the family parlor in the big old house. Many family members busied themselves in the kitchen, fixing a feast for people coming to the wake. Tables for eating lunch were set up under the big oak trees in the backyard. Most of the activity of the day centered around food.

I walked into the parlor to pay my respects with a handful of others who had recently arrived and were eventually on their way toward the kitchen. Thankfully, I was in the parlor when a great-grandson was viewing the body. At one point, the great-grandson pulled out a new block of Red Man chewing tobacco and nestled it into the chest pocket of the jacket on the deceased as he lay in the coffin. The great-grandson did this as he said to me, "A little something for Paw for the journey."

From the rural, old, and traditional, let me move to the modern and contemporary.

A friend, George, died in May 2020. The family opted for a Celebration of Life, not a traditional funeral. The celebration included a long video merging music and pictures from George's past. In some ways, it was almost as if George was being roasted. People showed up in Atlanta soccer colors; George was a diehard fan. The Celebration of Life was a truly festive affair focused on celebrating George. Everyone said it was perfect for him.

While I have gathered a few examples of funerals and grieving traditions from memory, the variations are much more extensive than my experience can articulate. Unique funerals and grief traditions exist across the country, to say nothing of the larger world. These subcultural traditions are ingrained in each of us. In moments of great joy or sadness, we find comfort in doing it "the way it is supposed to be done"—that is, in a way consistent with the subculture of our birth.

The Season of Life

The experience of grief is greatly influenced by the age of the deceased and the age of the one grieving.

Given that I have just begun my eighth decade of life, I could spend a good bit of time attending the visitations and funerals of people I have known. For those of us in our seventies, death is a normal part of life. We all hope to live another decade, but chances get increasingly slim the longer we live. As we advance in age, we become more comfortable with the death of others. We also increasingly make an important distinction about the quality of life; what is the point of a longer life if that longer life isn't worth living?

Those of us in the senior crowd do react strongly when young adults or children die; we tend to think of all they missed in not living longer.

Young adults, teenagers, and children see death differently. I remember the first significant death I experienced. Grandfather Pennell died after a relatively brief illness resulting from a life-long struggle with heart disease. I was a college student at the time. I remember feeling anxious but uncertain of exactly how I was supposed to react and feel about my grandfather's death. I was not particularly close to him; we moved away from Portsmouth when I was eleven, so I had not been around him much in the previous decade.

Most of the funeral and the days after that are foggy to me. I specifically remember being assigned to drive one of the cars from the funeral to the graveside. I was driving for an aunt and her two children. As I started driving the car from the church, my aunt began crying loudly. I sensed her deep sadness and was bewildered about how to respond. I thought, "Why am I not feeling like her?"

Of course, that was my unique experience, shaped by many influences I did not understand. Death tends to be a distant reality for the young, not so much for many of us.

We all tend to applaud the person who lives into their mid-nineties. When they die, we say, "They lived a full and rich life." We rarely refer to their deaths as a tragedy.

In the church communities I served in over the years, we always had a full house for two types of funerals: the funeral

of a much-loved older adult and the senseless death of a teenager or child.

Age influences grief. The age of the deceased matters
in terms of the grief that will be experienced by family and
friends. The age and experience of the person grieving are
equally important.

Religious Views

Most of us are familiar with the mantra at the family
reunion—do not bring up religion or politics. The sage advice
seeks to minimize conflict at the family gathering; conversations about politics and religion rarely change anyone's
views. It turns out that there is research that supports this
basic premise. In his book, *The Art and Science of Personality
Development*, Dan McAdams notes that religion and politics
tend to be rooted in one's worldview or deeply held values.
To ask someone to change their political or religious views is
to ask the individual to reconfigure the foundation of their
identity. A change in perspective rarely happens among those
with clear, deeply held views on politics or religion.

One's religious views heavily influence the experience of
grief.

Some evangelical Christians believe God directs every
aspect of a person's life. In the case of a tragic death, the
response might be, "We may not understand the why, but we
know this death is God's will." This is often their response to
the death of a two-year-old due to cancer or the death of a
sixteen-year-old in a tragic automobile accident: "It is God's
will." The person who holds to this worldview is willingly
locked into this response by their core convictions. Grief for
them is, therefore, an effort to shift responsibility for the death
of the loved one onto God. In some ways, this is grief denied.
The struggle for the individual then becomes a struggle to

reaffirm their worldview in the face of loss and disappointment. For most people in this religious sub-culture, their loss is experienced only in ways that are consistent with their overall worldview. In this tradition, the funeral service does not focus on loss or grief but becomes a celebration of God's providence and will, or a celebration of the deceased person's life. In either case, grief and loss are suspended, and emotions are channeled into celebration.

Long after the funeral, an individual may experience sadness at the deceased's absence, but the momentary sense of loss will be quickly soothed with, "Ah, but their death was God's will. I don't always understand, but I always trust God." Others with different religious traditions may view this as grief denied, but this approach seems to work well for those committed to this worldview.

Of course, there are exceptions. For some reared in this perspective, their sense of loss overwhelms their worldview, and they reach a conviction that the death of their loved one was not the will of God. This "new revelation" upsets their worldview, and these individuals are mostly going to find themselves in severe grief or profound grief. They may experience severe grief because this is the first time they have felt the full weight of grief without a supporting religious worldview as on previous occasions when their "it's God's will" perspective held. Most likely, this individual will tumble into profound grief because the death of this person has forced them to rearrange the foundation stones of their sense of self.

Other Christians who hold to a different perspective on the role God plays in everyday life will view the death of the two-year-old or sixteen-year-old differently. These Christians might shift grief and blame for the deceased's death to larger societal concerns: "If we Americans had spent more on cancer research (and less on bombs), this death could have been avoided," or, "We Americans must put a greater priority on educating teens not to drink and drive." Christians who are of this subculture are apt to emphasize the deceased as "in a better place," heaven. Of course, there is much discussion and disagreement in the Christian tradition regarding what happens immediately on death to the deceased: some embrace purgatory, others opt for the deceased in graves awaiting the Resurrection of the Dead, and others focus on Paul's admonishment, "absent from the body, present with the Lord." Christianity does not lack for diversity of opinions.

It is important to recognize that each Christian subcultural group will pick and choose the beliefs emphasized in their tradition regarding grief. As noted above regarding the way grief is processed, those in the "It's God's will" group tend to emphasize "God's will" even over the sense that the deceased is "in heaven." Meanwhile, those in the second subcultural set noted above tend to focus on the "better place" of heaven. Each group is attempting to move through grief holding to cherished values; those cherished values may or may not align with biblical or Christian theology.

Because Christianity is an exceedingly complex grouping of people, still others will embrace the sense of loss and grief in tragic deaths without appealing to a controlling worldview. These individuals will grasp a variety of core convictions as they manage their way through grief. While these Christians will have a less clearly defined pathway through grief, they will move through grief anchored to a hodge-podge of convictions and unique perspectives developed throughout their lives. In the end, their foundations tend to prove adequate for the challenge.

In describing grief attached to various Christian subcultures, I have offered general ideas of how grief is dealt with depending on slightly differing values (beliefs). In truth, there are hundreds, if not thousands, of ways Christians deal with loss and grief. I am merely suggesting a few to provide a clue to the complexity offered in Christian tradition.

Jewish traditions around death and dying provide a clear context for the experience of grief. While there is considerable diversity in the larger Jewish community (Orthodox, Reformed, and non-practicing), there is a generally accepted pattern to grief and mourning as follows:

Following death, the body is washed. If the deceased is a man, then men wash the body. If the deceased is a woman, then women wash the body. The body is dressed in a simple white burial shroud. There is great care to respect the body of the deceased. Someone guards the body between the washing and the funeral; bodies are never left alone. This is not a prolonged period, as Jewish funerals tend to happen shortly after death. The traditional Jewish funeral is a brief affair often featuring black ribbons symbolically torn as an expression of grief. Male members of the family carry the casket. Jewish burial customs dictate that family members place dirt on top of the casket, symbolizing their acceptance of the death. Shiva, a traditional mourning period, lasts seven days (sometimes shorter). The Mourner's Kaddish is a prayer traditionally recited daily for thirty days or up to eleven months, depending on the person's relationship to the deceased.

The Jewish practice is relatively well-defined. The rituals associated with death and grief provide a framework for personal expressions of grief; there is always something to do physically/emotionally. It also has well-established time-frames for types of expressions of grief. Before the funeral, the tearing of cloth is a physical and psychological exercise for expressing grief. For a prescribed period (seven days, thirty days, up to eleven months), specific prayers are recited daily to process grief.

The Jewish tradition provides a well-worn approach to experiencing and processing grief. If the individual embraces the Jewish worldview, then the pathway through grief is well-defined. Those who are non-practicing Jews or marginally Jewish may have a different experience as they do not philosophically embrace traditional Jewish practice.

Islamic funeral and grief traditions center on two primary objectives: to provide safe passage to the individual who has expired and to provide comfort as loved ones and the larger community grapple with the loss that death brings.

The deceased's family is responsible for speeding the soul on its journey. Thus, the funeral is often conducted on the day of death or soon after. The family performs personal care of the deceased, including washing, perfuming, and grooming. After enshrouding the body, the family invites close friends and family to spend time with it before the funeral. While there are detailed rituals regarding the care of the body and the funeral, typically, these matters are left to the discretion of the family.

The entire community is invited to the funeral, and everyone is expected to come unless prevented by health or some other significant issue. The service follows strictly the Salat al-Janazah, an established set of prayers and funeral order. At the grave site, the deceased's body is placed directly on the soil (where practical) and then turned so the body is on its right side, facing Mecca. Each person present then tosses three handfuls of earth into the grave.

In Islam, one's earthly life is but one stage of life; after death, the individual goes to heaven, where their fate is determined. If the individual is proven worthy, they are rewarded with eternal life in heaven and its seven levels. If they are not worthy, then they are condemned to Jahannam (hell), a grave-like existence awaiting a chance to be redeemed or forgiven when all the dead will be resurrected.

An Islamic funeral provides significant support to the grieving family. The larger community provides food to the grieving family for three days, sometimes up to forty days. In the case of a widow, the larger group is responsible for aiding her in observing four months and ten days of mourning. During this time, she is not to leave her home. Displays of grief are always modest and subdued to show the strength of one's faith and trust in God.

Practicing Muslims pray to God five times daily, creating a sense that God is an active participant in their lives. Life, in whatever state an individual exists, is under the rule and providence of God. While an individual's death is cause for grief and sadness, the deceased remains under the watchful eye of a loving yet firm deity.

The Muslim tradition provides a clear framework for understanding loss and embracing grief. Its timeframe for grief establishes parameters with lots of support from the larger community. In this way, it also creates relatively clear timeframes for the ending of specific rituals related to the grieving process. These historic rituals aid the grieving journey and tend to conclude the period of active grieving.

The institution of slavery heavily influenced African American grief traditions; these modern traditions had their beginnings during the era of enslavement. On plantations, an enslaved person's death was viewed in two different ways.

While the owner or owner's family may have had emotional ties to the deceased, the death meant a vital resource was depleted. If the death occurred during a harvest, the owner needed to do everything possible to keep the other slaves in the field working the harvest; he could not afford an extended work stoppage for any reason.

The enslaved community had lost a treasured family member. Given the constraints of slavery, grieving was compartmentalized: One worked the field while they grieved.

The unique context of American slavery gave rise to a unique grieving experience among modern African Americans in the United States, especially in geographical regions where slavery was prominent.

One of the best summaries of this tradition is by Kami Fletcher, a professor at Albright College. Fletcher mentions several significant characteristics of grieving and funeral traditions for African Americans: "The Homegoing is the ceremonial send-off of the deceased to heaven." Time is generally suspended at a Homegoing, and it is acceptable for songs, hymns, eulogies, sermons, prayers, and tributes to run long. "The hymns, gospel songs and the designated solos frame the Homegoing," Fletcher writes, "encouraging public displays of grief."

In this tradition, the casket is almost always open. When people enter the church, they pass by the open casket and then by a line of family members; sometimes, this sequence is repeated at the end of the service when people depart. Viewing the body is a significant issue in this tradition, and the deceased will be decked out in the very finest attire possible; in the context of eighteenth-century slavery, lying in a casket was the only time "Black folks were allowed to present themselves not as someone's slave." This context generated the colloquialism "casket sharp."

Music is always a central focus of this tradition. Solos and choir presentations often include clapping by the audience and generally create an environment for public expressions of grief. Homegoing music tends to focus on themes of going home, liberation, the joys of heaven, and the release from sorrow and struggle.

Funeral programs are elaborate documents with pages of high-resolution photographs and lengthy tributes about the deceased. They also include a detailed list of the elements of the Homegoing and introductory and lengthy sketches of those on the program. The program is designed as a tribute and a keepsake from the Homegoing.

> The repast is the literal feast that follows the burial after the Homegoing. The food is prepared to perfection and prepared in bulk for all funeral goers to eat-and-eat two or three times over. . . . The repast, a feast shared between the bereaved, is a way to get back to eating, a way back to normalcy . . . there is a purposeful shift in mood, a shift to a celebration, sometimes even a party.[1]

Religious belief and one's specific worldview create parameters for the journey of grief. If an individual is committed to those parameters, then their grieving process tends to work itself out in traditional and well-established patterns. It works for those committed to that worldview.

The brief, brief survey of practices in the Abrahamic faiths noted above just touches the surface of the complexity and diversity in religious faith. I did not mention the Eastern traditions in the Christian Church, or Hindu or Buddhist or the hundreds of other faith traditions.

The point I am making is simple and straightforward. For those committed to a particular faith tradition or sub-tradition, their tradition is a major influencer in the way they will experience and process grief.

I would also add a note about "Nones"; these are the people who increasingly identify with none of the faith traditions. Nones have worldviews and deeply held values. If their worldview is deeply held, then they, too, have a framework for interpreting dying and processing grief.

---

1. Dr. Kami Fletcher, "7 Elements of African American Mourning Practices & Burial Traditions," *Talk Death*, February 8, 2021, https://www.talkdeath.com/7-elements-of-african-american-mourning-practices-burial-traditions/.

In this chapter, I have outlined several perspectives which have a direct influence on the experience of grief. I hope this chapter has simply opened the reader's consciousness to consider any number of influencers to grief. I have listed influencers which I have noted over my personal experience. My experience is limited when we appreciate the multitude of cultural and religious traditions around the globe.

Chapter 5

The Brain and Grief

"Now, that is a face only a mother could love." The brunt of this old saying was typically an old country boy with less than dashing facial features. Unknown to whoever first spoke those words, there is science behind the saying. During giving birth, oxytocin is released into the bloodstream by the pituitary gland. This hormone fosters a bond between the mother and child[1] that is strengthened with skin-to-skin contact, breastfeeding, and a host of experiences in the months after birth. The bonding between a mother and child is a byproduct of our evolutionary past and is characteristic of many species. The mother-child bond includes affection, protection, and love. This bonding, originating in the release of oxytocin, makes permanent changes in the brain.[2]

In this chapter, I want to address the brain's role in grief, but first, another well-known saying.

All my days, I have heard people say, "depression is caused by a chemical imbalance in the brain." It is more complex than that, though chemicals do play a role in depression. It is not that the level of one chemical is low or another is high; it is far more complex. Some people have a genetic sensitivity to depression, and several centers in the brain play essential roles in depression. Explaining depression is not simple chemistry.

---

1. Howard E. LeWine, "Oxytocin: The Love Hormone," *Harvard Health Publishing*, June 13, 2023, https://health.harvard.edu/mind-and-mood/oxytocin-the-love-hormone.

2. Ibid.

Rather, there are multiple ingredients and dimensions to it. The saying about "chemical imbalances" is an unsophisticated way of noting that the one suffering from depression is at the mercy of forces beyond their control as it is something that cannot be cured with a more positive attitude.

The brain is a player in our grief.

The two examples cited above are familiar. They illustrate ways the brain is working independent of any conscious choice by the owner of that brain. During birth, there is an "automatic" rush of oxytocin, much as is experienced in all mammals at birth. Changing the brain's chemical mixture is not something an individual is able to influence, let alone control.

In our conversation going forward, I need to make an important distinction between the conscious part of human existence (the Self) and the brain. At times, our brain seems to have a mind of its own; it does things without the Self knowing about it. Thankfully, the brain keeps us breathing even though the Self doesn't make decisions about breathing or our heart rate. The brain and body seem, at times, to function automatically—they do what needs to be done without involving conscious choices by the Self. In some ways, independent of specific choices by the Self, the brain is self-regulating.

Some of us know about the experience of shock. It can happen because of physical injury. Because of an automobile accident, a significant fall, or an injury around power equipment, we suffer a traumatic injury—and the brain responds with shock: we don't tell our brain to do this; it just does it on its own. Shock, a mechanism developed over the course of our evolutionary history, insulates us emotionally and psychologically from traumatic injury.

A similar sense of shock happens with emotional loss. Many of us who have experienced the sudden death of a spouse know well the mental fog that tends to result when we are first confronted with the reality of death. Without the Self deciding, the brain springs into action on our behalf, or else the magnitude of our emotional loss might completely overwhelm us.

The brain is a player in our grief; the brain's self-regulating function does not stop when the initial shock of death dissipates.

There is a good bit of research going on related to grief and the functioning of the brain. Mary-Frances O'Conner is a pioneer in the neuroscience of grief. She directs the Grief, Loss, and Social Stress (GLASS) Lab at the University of Arizona. In research for this manuscript, I discovered her book *The Grieving Brain: The Surprising Science of How We Learn from Love and Loss.* O'Conner's research is based on a variety of methodologies focused on scans of the brain and grief.[3] She is a neuroscientist and a psychologist. Hers is an empirical approach based on hard science. David S. Moore is a professor of psychology at Pitzer College and Claremont Graduate University and author of *The Developing Genome: An Introduction to Behavioral Epigenetics.* Moore's work focuses on the intersection between psychology and biology with a specific interest in understanding the way epigenetics interplay with human behavior.

In an introductory book like this one, I am not going to summarize the research of the authors noted above. This would take us too far from the primary interest of this book. I will provide quotes and insights from their work that are especially applicable to our topic.

Epigenetics refers to how genetic material is activated or deactivated—that is, expressed—in different contexts or

---

3. Mary-Frances O'Connor, *The Grieving Brain: The Surprising Science of How We Learn from Love and Loss* (New York: Harper, 2022).

situations. Think of it like this: DNA works like a light switch that can be turned on or off. Even better, DNA works like a dimmer switch; it can be turned on just a little bit, a moderate amount, a lot, full-blast, or any amount in between. How active a DNA segment is depends on its epigenetic state, which depends on factors like its context.[4]

Chemical markers in the brain establish patterns that vary how much one gene is turned on and how much another is limited. Epigenetic changes do not change our DNA but regulate how many of our genes are turned on and how much they are turned on. Epigenetics is injecting a new element into the old conversation about nature and nurture. We now know that nurture (environment and experiences) creates chemical markers in the brain and influences our individual expression of nature (which genes are turned on or off and the degree to which they are turned on or off).

Epigenetic changes in the brain (think neuropathways) can be altered. Many couples experience bonding in courtship and marriage; that is, epigenetic markers are made in the brain, and neuropathways are established related to that other special person.[5]

If you are new to epigenetics, all of this probably sounds strange, even outlandish. Most of us grew up with the nature vs nurture conversation. Are my individual actions based on my DNA, or have nurturing influences over my lifetime created the pattern that explains my actions? The nature vs nurture conversation is almost second nature to all of us. Of course, the way this conversation has been framed has an important underlying assumption—that there are only two

---

4. David S. Moore, *The Developing Genome: An Introduction to Behavioral Epigenetics* (Oxford: Oxford University, 2015), 14.

5. O'Connor, *Grieving Brain*, 112.

options. That is, the underlying assumption is that individual behaviors must be rooted mainly in either nature or nurture.

Did you experience immediate resistance to my suggestion when I introduced the epigenetic option? Why? Before we understood anything about epigenetics, we would reply, "I have read a good bit about nature versus nurture. I have never heard about epigenetics. What is the scientific basis for epigenetics? You will have to convince me if you think I am buying epigenetics."

Some would say their resistance to this new idea is rooted in their intellect, their knowledge of information stored in the folds of the brain and accessed by the Self. That tends to be the way we think about the Self and the brain. The Self is in charge, and the brain is simply a storage bank of information. Of course, this is incorrect.

Based on previous experience and education, our brains develop neuropathways around specific topics; thus, we approach the nature versus nurture conversation via those well-established pathways. To embrace a new idea like epigenetics requires us to not only engage our intellect but also to begin unwinding neuropathways in the brain. As it took time to develop those neuropathways, it takes time to unwind them.

I have enjoyed following news about the relatively new James Webb space telescope. The telescope's findings are re-writing our understanding of the earliest beginnings of the universe. At the bare minimum, the telescope is forcing a re-evaluation of the Big Bang theory as to how the universe began. Having lived with the Big Bang theory all my life, I find I am resistant to embracing this "new-fangled" approach to the origin of our universe. My resistance is composed of more than my intellect; I have to deal with established neuropathways in my brain.[6]

These epigenetic markers or neuropathways can be very stable and entrenched. Initially, most researchers thought of epigenetic markers as existing during a person's lifetime; that is, they thought the markers were 'wiped clean' at death and were not inheritable. That view changed as more research proved that some markers were passed down to progeny via the germline.[7] The germline is the designation of the fertility process (sperm, egg, etc.) used by scientists. In some cases, epigenetic markers are passed along the male lineage.[8]

For example, Ty, Doug, and Jake (three male generations) despise fruit. They refuse it at every offer. In fact, Doug has a terrible time peeling an orange for his granddaughter to the point he gags and feels like he will throw up. Prior to epigenetics, we would simply suggest that the men in this family line had been influenced psychologically by their fathers. Each was just trying to be like his father in embracing a dislike of fruit. We now know epigenetic markers sometimes are passed down from generation to generation. A firm conclusion that Ty's, Doug's, and Jake's issues with fruit are a result of epigenetic markers would require specific research on the three of them; even so, it sure seems suspicious given the research evidence we already know from others.[9] To speculate in an area unrelated to the trio above, might sensitivity to alcohol across generations be explained by inherited epigenetic markers as well?[10]

---

6. Moore, *Developing Genome*, 56, 63, 106.

7. Ibid., 169.

8. Ibid., 182.

9. Ibid., 184–186.

10. Ibid., 132, 141–142.

Established neuropathways can be very helpful and beneficial.

Many married people, or parents, are familiar with a thought randomly popping into consciousness, "Where is my husband/wife?" or "where are my children?" Why do these random thoughts just pop into our heads? The brain has established epigenetic markers, neuropathways, and the brain is doing its work to keep us aware of essential concerns. Psychiatrist Mardi Horowitz called these intrusive thoughts[11] and described them as happening more often when an individual is under stress.

Occasionally, parents are surprised by a behavior of their child. Maybe they discover their daughter has been lying to them, or their son has been spending way too much time at a local teen hangout. The parent's brain is, thus, under increased stress related to a child. The frequency of intrusive thoughts about the child will be greatly increased by the brain without a conscious decision by the Self.

In the case of loss and grief, cascading intrusive thoughts are the brain's attempt to reconcile itself to a new reality: the death of an individual.[12] The intrusive thoughts are manufactured by the brain and sent to the Self. The Self is not generating intrusive thoughts.

You have heard the adage "You can't teach an old dog new tricks." Typically, this adage is invoked by an older adult who is basically saying, "I am too old and tired to learn something new (often related to technology)." From an epigenetic perspective, the individual is saying, "It is just too hard to change the well-established neuropathways in my brain."

As this is an important insight, it is worth repeating for clarity. In addition to the involuntary work our brains do

---

11. O'Connor, *Grieving Brain*, 126.
12. Ibid., 130.

(heart rate, etc.), our brains also have established neuropathways (epigenetics) to understand and cope with the larger world around us. Although these epigenetic changes and neuropathways are well established, they can be changed throughout life. Even so, changing neuropathways and epigenetic expressions can be difficult and take time and effort—sometimes a lot of time and even more effort.

A mundane example may be helpful. In the United States, we drive on the right side of the road. We have developed the habit of driving on the right side of the road; in our brains (over the years), we have developed epigenetic markers and neuropathways consistent with driving on the right side of the road. In other countries, you drive on the left side of the road; my neuropathways almost had me writing "the wrong side of the road." When you visit another country and drive for the first time on the left side of the road, you notice all kinds of mental moments: the first time you experience another car coming in the opposite direction and going by you on the right side of the car you are driving. Often, in this situation, people tend to overcompensate and favor the extreme left edge of the road. Every time you start up the car and head out for a drive (in the other country), you must remind yourself on which side to drive.

Another example. My father smoked cigarettes for over twenty years before stopping. I remember him smoking when I was a child. He always kept his pack of cigarettes in his shirt pocket. A dozen and more years after he stopped smoking, he would occasionally reach toward his pocket for a cigarette. I remember him reaching for a cigarette in my presence when I was a teenager. He looked at me and said, "After all these years, I still reach for a cigarette; don't ever start smoking."

Why did he keep reaching for a cigarette long after he stopped smoking? It could have been because of well-established neuropathways in the brain.[13]

Women who shave their legs often start in the exact same place on their legs every time they shave. Please do not ask a man using a safety razor to begin shaving at a different place on his face; typically, he will have more nicks than you can count. Before we knew about epigenetics, we would ascribe these repeated patterns as habits. Apparently, there is science behind these habits of ours.

Every year at my annual Medicare physical, my doctors say something like, "I want you to draw the face of a clock showing 3:30." I respond by drawing the face of a clock with two hands—a shorter one and a longer one. Of course, my granddaughter, responding to the same question, would draw a digital clock. As a younger child, she would wake up very early in the morning. Her parents established the rule she had to stay in bed until a certain time. So, I asked her one morning, "What time did you get up this morning?" She replied with, "six, dot, dot, zero, zero." My granddaughter, smart as a whip, has to think pretty hard about drawing an old-fashioned clock showing 3:30. With regard to clock faces, her neuropathways and mine are different.

The brain is a significant player in our experience of grief.

The death of a spouse brings sadness and loss and requires us to deal with the well-established neuropathways in our brain built around a person who is no longer with us. Part of grief is simply coping with loss; another part is dealing with the complexity of well-established neuropathways that are no longer appropriate, given the death we grieve.[14]

---

13. Moore, *Developing Genome*, 183.
14. Ibid., 106.

Many of us who have grieved a significant loss know well the mental fog, disorientation, and confusion that come with grief. Until epigenetics, all we could say about these realities was, "It's part of grief." Now, we can acknowledge it is partly grief and partly well-worn neuropathways having to adjust.[15]

I need to pause now and acknowledge that what I am writing is a bit revolutionary. Today, professionals tend to think of grief from their areas of expertise. So, theologians/pastors have a take on loss and grief, as do neuroscientists and counselors. I am attempting to offer an interdisciplinary perspective on grief. In this chapter, I attempt to bring the insights of neuroscientists into pastoral and personal conversations about grief. This is also a good place to acknowledge that the emerging field of epigenetics is a bit controversial even though the research seems solid. While professors wrote several of the books most referenced in this chapter of psychology, other psychologists argue it is too early to endorse some of the conclusions of epigenetics. While their resistance must be taken seriously, it must also be noted that epigenetics has the potential to upend traditional perspectives in psychology built on the insights of Sigmund Freud and a long line of others. The modern field of psychology emerged well before technical advances with brain scans and information about epigenetics. As the scientific weight of epigenetic research grows, the field of psychology is in for significant change.

For my own part, I think epigenetic markers and established but changeable neuropathways are active aspects of grief. Grief is certainly about loss and sadness. Yet, loss and sadness do not explain all of what goes on in the experience of grief. A significant part of grief is impacted by established neuropathways in the brain. Before my own experience of

---

15. O'Connor, *Grieving Brain*, 155–56.

significant grief, I counted myself among those who hold traditional psychological views about grief: the mental fog and trouble with mental focus are caused by sadness and loss. Having traveled the road of significant grief, I changed my mind.

I think this struggle to embrace epigenetic insights and brain research as it relates to grief is like old attitudes about depression. For too long, people thought depression was just extended sadness, and the fundamental therapy for it centered on conversations about how the patient felt. Now, we know depression is related to concrete things going on in the brain, and talking is not the most effective therapy. In significant grief, something concrete is happening in the brain; epigenetics is a helpful explanation.

We are venturing into the arena described *as the new science of bereavement.*[16] One of the most important studies in this new science was conducted in the 1990s and concluded with a scientific report in 2000: Changing Lives of Older Couples (CLOC). This longitudinal study of over fifteen hundred older adults has been very influential in the field of bereavement. George Bonanno developed an empirical model of grieving over time from this database.[17] In Bonanno's case, he was particularly interested in the connection between depression and grief. His work identified four major trajectories of grief over four years.

Of the fifteen hundred individuals who lost a spouse, 66 percent were identified as *resilient*—they never experienced depression related to the death of a spouse. This was a surprising number as many professional counselors tended to think those avoiding depression would be significantly

---

16. Ibid., xv.

17. Bonanno, *Other Side of Sadness*, 8–11; O'Connor, *Grieving Brain*, 81–88.

lower. Those who struggled with depression before the death of a spouse saw their anxiety and depression grow slowly over forty-eight months following the death of a spouse; this group represented 14.5 percent of the study and was identified as *chronic depression*. Of the study group, 9.1 percent experienced new depression because of the death of a spouse; these were identified as *chronic grief*. Of this group, their depression peaked six months after the death, began a more significant decline after eighteen months, and dissipated by forty-eight months. The last group, *depressed improved*, experienced significant depression at the death of a spouse but were no longer depressed six months after the death of a spouse.

This study is noteworthy for several reasons. The identification of four trajectories is significant. The fact that 66 percent of those in the study experienced "normal grief" and escaped depression is very significant. Researchers tend to focus more sharply on the 33 percent of people who experience problematic grief. In the study, nearly half of those who experienced problematic grief were struggling with depression before the death of a spouse. About one-third of the group experienced initial depression symptoms at the death of a spouse, but those symptoms had subsided by eighteen months.

The Rotterdam Study is another study often quoted by bereavement researchers. The Dutch study focused on what it identified as complicated grief in 150 older adults. This sample was compared to 615 bereaved people who did not manifest complicated grief (the normal grief group) and to 4,731 nonbereaved people. The study did not include those suffering from depression. The results noted that those suffering from complicated grief had less brain volume than the other two groups. Those experiencing complicated grief also tended to score slightly lower on cognitive ability tests.

For the 150 people who experienced complicated grief, their slightly lower cognitive abilities may have made them more susceptible to complicated grief, or their complicated grief may have affected their cognitive abilities.[18] Another important result was that 615 of the 765 who experienced grief did not manifest complicated grief—80 percent experienced "normal" grief.

Based on the Rotterdam study data, Paul Boelen and Maarten Eisma made several important contributions related to ruminations in grieving.[19] Rumination is the process of remembering over and over events related to the loss of a loved one. For example, those who grieve often replay in their minds events and conversations related to the death of a loved one; they might do this over and over every day for months. The ruminations focused on one of five areas: emotional reactions to the loss, unfairness of the death, consequences of the death, reactions of others to the grief of the one grieving, and "what-ifs" related to the loved one's death.[20]

The researchers also noted a correlation between the frequency of ruminations and the need to avoid feeling the depth of the loss. That is, the brain invites us to replay events, conversations, and experiences related to the death as a way of holding the loss at bay emotionally.[21] It is easier to busy oneself with reciting a litany of events and conversations than to face fully the emotions of the loss itself. In effect, the brain keeps us busy with ruminations as we slowly embrace the utter emotional weight of the loss. As peaceful acceptance of the emotional loss is embraced, the ruminations begin declining significantly.

---

18. O'Connor, *Grieving Brain*, 93–96.
19. Ibid., 151.
20. Ibid.
21. Ibid., 155.

As I conclude this chapter on the brain and grief, it will be helpful to reconfirm several key points.

First, it is imperative that we distinguish between the Self and our brain. The brain has many ongoing tasks that escape the Self's notice. The brain regulates our heart and keeps bodily functions operating normally. The brain also does unique things without asking the Self for permission. We noted the role of shock in physical and emotional injuries.

Second, it takes the brain some time to readjust to the new reality that a significant person died. The Self has no choice but to embrace this new reality as there are decisions to be made about a funeral, family gatherings, etc. Because of the well-established neuropathways and epigenetic adaptations of the brain, it takes the brain some time to adjust to the new reality of the loved one's death. Historically, we thought mental fog, disorientation, and trouble with focus were simply part of loss and grief. Now we understand they partly exist because the brain is trying to unwind neuropathways and create new ones.

Third, the brain generates *intrusive thoughts* and invites ruminations as a way of trying to adjust to the death of a loved one. *Intrusive thoughts* are generated by the brain more often because of the stress of loss. The one grieving is prompted by the brain about the deceased loved one as it struggles to embrace the new reality of the loved one's death; after the brain has adjusted to the reality of the death, *intrusive thoughts* about the loved one are greatly reduced. In the case of ruminations, the brain invites ruminations to insulate the individual from the full emotional weight of the loss. Busying oneself with remembrances about the death, funeral, loss, etc., is a way of holding the loss's intensity at bay.

Fourth, more than 66 percent of people with normal cognitive abilities and no history of mental illness will navigate grief without significant complications (depression, prolonged grief disorder, complicated grief, etc.). One study suggested 80 percent of people will experience normal grief.

Fifth, those who experience depression at the death of, and because of, a loved one typically are over their depression eighteen months after the death of the loved one.

Sixth, the subculture one grows up in imprints its distinctive perspective on the brain. In an earlier chapter, I mentioned the African American perspective on death and grief, especially in relation to funeral traditions. The African American worldview rooted in the South imprints itself on the brain via epigenetic adaptations and neuropathways. For these African Americans experiencing grief, it is altogether natural to process their loss through that specific worldview, consistent with their values and neuropathways. It is important to also note the struggle if someone attempts to process grief in a way inconsistent with the worldview in which they were reared and contrary to neuropathways created by that worldview. As adults, some people embrace a worldview that is contrary to that of their childhood; this can complicate the experience of grief.

As a postscript to this chapter, let me acknowledge the philosophical, theological, and moral issues that arise from a distinction between the Self and the brain. We can all imagine the accused saying in court, "My brain made me do it." Historically, in the United States, we have made legal exceptions for people suffering from impulse disorders and temporary mental illness, both of which suggest a disconnect between the brain and the responsible Self.

Chapter 6

Ways to Process Grief

Images, or how we think about ourselves and the circumstances of our world, are important, even life-shaping. This is certainly true regarding loss and grief.

As I noted in an earlier chapter, many of us hold to a worldview, faith, or life perspective that helps us deal with loss and grief. If that perspective is deeply held to the point of being part of the foundation stones of how we think of ourselves (personal identity), then those traditions will be exceedingly helpful for us as we grieve. There is no one philosophical perspective on loss and grief that makes the journey easy; rather, many pathways have been well-worn over decades and centuries. These dozens of pathways can serve individuals well.

I begin this chapter on ways to process grief by asking about the reader's sense of connection to a worldview. To state it straightforwardly, if one is deeply committed to a worldview, then grieve according to the tenets of that worldview.

Of course, many of my readers are not deeply committed to one specific faith tradition or worldview. In that case, I offer most of the rest of this book. What follows is intended to be helpful to those without specific faith traditions or worldviews nestled near their sense of identity.

Loss and grief impose unique stress on individuals. This unique stress can expose fault lines in our worldview or emotional sense of self, which typically are unimportant in day-to-day life. Having officiated several hundred funerals,

I have seen this subtility exposed in many ways. If a family member wanted to deliver the eulogy in the funeral service, I would typically talk with them about the unique stress of loss and grief. I would advise that when a family member stands up to offer the eulogy, they often are surprised by the welling of emotion inside themselves. I've seen it dozens of times: a confident family member with experience in public speaking rises and walks to the podium to deliver the eulogy—three sentences into the well-prepared eulogy, they become over-whelmed with emotion and can hardly get a word out.

A journey through grief requires a careful strategy.

In the journey with grief, sleep is required. In the wake of a loved one's death, getting a normal night's sleep can be a real chore. Many grieving people have trouble sleeping. The most often complaint is, "I can't turn off my brain." That is, the brain seems caught in a constant replay of the circum-stances around the loved one's death or replay around the implications of the death. As noted in the earlier chapter about the brain, some of this is related to the brain's effort to insulate the individual from the full weight of the loss. Sleep deprivation will greatly complicate the grief journey. Grief brings a mental fog all its own. If a lack of sleep is added, then it is going to be nearly impossible to navigate with grief.

In my case, two Tylenol PMs every night thirty minutes before going to bed helped me fall asleep. This worked 90 percent of the time. If it had not worked, I would have tried other over-the-counter sleep aids. If needed, I would have asked my doctor to prescribe something. Getting a night's sleep is a big deal when dealing with deep grief. Thankfully, there are many nonaddictive options available.

Exercise is important on the journey of grief. Keeping your body moving is important. In the wake of a loved one's death, there tends to be a lot of sitting around. As quickly as possible, the grieving person needs to reestablish a level of physical activity like that before the loved one's death; in fact, increasing the level of activity by 10 percent to 20 percent is highly advisable. Making physical activity a priority will pay rich dividends on the journey with grief.

Getting clear about what is happening to you in your journey with grief is essential if you are to move toward a better place. In an early chapter of this book, I identified four categories: non-grief, grief, severe grief, and profound grief. These four categories can provide much-needed clarity; it is helpful to articulate what is happening to you in your journey. Most people who experience severe grief or profound grief do not have a vocabulary or a framework to describe what they are experiencing. They can certainly hurt and feel deep sadness but have no clue how their experience compares to others or if what they are thinking and feeling is within normal parameters. The four categories provide a framework for individuals to see themselves and their journey in a larger context. In addition, the chapter on the brain and grief offers neuroscientific information about the grieving brain; some of our struggle in grief is based on the brain's efforts to find a new normal, to unwind neuropathways, and to create new ones—all under significant stress. Those who experience mild grief may not notice struggles with neuropathways in the brain. Significant grief increases stress and will more fully involve struggles related to neuropathways in the brain.

For those in the grip of profound grief, it is immensely helpful to acknowledge they are feeling legitimate sadness at the death of a significant person in their life and to recognize their loved one's death has stirred a pot in the arena of mental health. This pot has been brewing for a long time and drifted under the radar of self-understanding. While acknowledging that grief has touched a mental health concern can be a bit disconcerting, it sure is nice to be able to parse out different threads in the grief journey. Simply knowing you are facing severe grief interwoven with a mental health concern is extremely helpful.

Many medical patients are relieved to finally get a diagnosis, even if the news is less than hopeful. A diagnosis helps patients know where they stand, and a pathway forward becomes increasingly clear. Clarity is extremely helpful.

In the chapter on Influences, I attempted to describe the nature of a person's grief. For instance, it must be helpful for Sentimental Sam to know that his grief is influenced by his tender-hearted nature and the unsatisfying relationship he shared with his father. It is not hard to imagine a conversation Sentimental Sam might have with himself.

Yep, being tender-hearted as I am, I am simply going to feel some things more deeply than others. This wonderful ability that I naturally possess has benefited my friends and helped me develop professional relationships. But "the gift" has a downside—I can experience deep emotional reactions to loss. It is my nature.

Yet, for me, there is this other piece to my grief. As in life, I kept bumping into this inner disappointment in the relationship I shared—or didn't share—with my dad. I desperately wanted him to accept me for who I was and am. Of course, that isn't going to happen. It was never going to happen, even if my dad lived another thirty years. My dad just wasn't capable of appreciating and affirming me as a person. While that failure hurt me, ultimately, it was my dad's flaw and his loss.

This kind of internal conversation, decoding thoughts and emotions, can only be helpful in the grief process. It helps one get a handle on what often appears as a rudderless experience with no meaning or direction. One of the most disconcerting parts of significant grief is that often, the one grieving has no clue what is happening to them.

Articulating what is going on in one's heart is essential to navigating grief. You cannot get a handle on what you cannot name or describe.

In her book *The Grieving Brain*, Mary-Frances O'Conner mentioned the importance of rumination. O'Conner wrote, "The mind ruminates when it cannot resolve the discrepancy between its current state, such as feeling down, and its desired state, such as feeling happy or content."[1]

In the context of grief, we are saddened by the loss of a loved one and long for the sadness to dissipate. Rumination, remembering and reciting the past over and over, becomes an activity to help the brain and the 'Self' to reconcile emotionally to a new reality.

In 2016, when I was facing my profound grief, I was not aware of the "new science of bereavement"; O'Conner's book was published in 2022. Consequently, I was unaware of how epigenetics and neuropathways play a part in grief. In truth, then, I was pretty much flying blind. While literature on the subject was plentiful, not much of it was helpful for me. Sometimes, in our ignorance, we find a healthy discipline despite ourselves.

As the need for ruminations about my wife's death seemed pressing upon me, I developed a discipline to embrace ruminations within parameters. Every morning, without fail, I devoted an hour to an hour-and-a-half to rumination, or as I called it at the time, processing my grief. My intent was to have a dedicated timeframe for rumination. In the first few weeks, this discipline didn't work particularly well, as I ruminated throughout the day. By week three, probably 80 percent of my ruminations were experienced during the designated timeframe. Prioritizing this dedicated timeframe

---

1. Ibid., 146–57, 150.

for rumination meant that after weeks, I could be more productive at work.

By the end of the second month, most of my ruminations were happening during the designated timeframe I had set aside. By the fifth month after my wife's death, I was ruminating for an hour or so every day, down from an hour and a half to two hours. The content of my ruminations also changed a bit. At first, many of my ruminations centered on finding my wife on the floor and the events that unfolded that night. As time passed, I ruminated less about that and focused more on the memorial services, the day the kids came to help me go through my wife's things, or how many trailer loads we carried off to a worthy cause. The farther I was removed from my wife's death, the less time I spent crying and just being overwhelmed—and the more I felt as if I was going to be OK.

Somewhere in the seventh month after my wife's death, I spent a Saturday morning moving mulch. As I was finishing up and spreading the last wheel borrow of the dump-truck mountain of mulch that had been delivered the day before, I realized I had not spent an hour ruminating at the beginning of the day. It was the first day I missed my routine of ruminating.

By the ninth month, I wasn't feeling an urgency about rumination. I decided to stop the regular rumination routine. After that, periods of rumination were less frequent and much less intense.

The extended time with ruminations helped me a great deal. In my opinion, the best part of the day was devoted to processing my grief. In addition, the routine was very helpful. Adding more structure to my day helped me feel as if I was getting back in charge of my day and life.

In the face of severe grief, it is important to get control of something. Of course, all I was trying to do was corral processing grief into a two-hour window, and it took me three weeks to manage it with some level of success. In the face of grief, any little victory is still a victory.

Realistic expectations are important for those who experience severe or profound grief. The intensity of grief subsides with time, but it takes a lot of time. For those deeply affected by grief, one needs to think of making progress in terms of months and years. In some regards, we learn to live with grief, recognizing it will never really go away. We adapt to its presence and learn how to keep it from dominating our world. I have, at times, described grief as ocean waves—they swell, break, and wash over us. Then it starts all over again; the waves just keep coming. In time we learn to manage our reaction to the waves, and eventually, they become less distracting and emotionally crippling. The waves may get smaller over time, but that takes a lot of time.

Processing grief takes time and energy. It helps if you are prepared for the journey.

Disciplines can be helpful in working with grief. The story in an earlier chapter about my friend who visited his son's grave every Sunday (and talking with him) might have been disturbing. Still, the routine of each week probably made a significant difference in the gentleman's progress with grief.

Grief management became part of his weekly ritual, part of his life. He worked on his grief just like he worked at his job. Personal rituals can be very effective and helpful in working through grief. In my case, I dedicated an hour to an hour and a half each morning to processing my grief. As a strong introvert, I have talked to myself and entertained myself during all seasons of my life. I fell into a pattern of talking out loud to myself, and I guess the universe, every day. I talked out loud, giving verbal expression to what I was thinking and feeling. I talked to myself. I talked to my deceased wife. I talked to God. My goal was to voice to whatever I was thinking and feeling at the moment. While this discipline produced no revelations or breakthroughs, it helped to take an edge off my grief.

Extroverts might find my discipline unhelpful. However, they might benefit from talking with others in group settings about their personal experiences with grief. The discipline needs to fit the personality.

Some people find rituals around anniversary dates helpful: the month anniversary of the death, the sixth month anniversary, the first anniversary (year), or multiple years. I never found this of much use, but others clearly do.

Professional expertise can also be helpful in working through grief. Counselors, mental health professionals, or people who have experienced our particular type of grief can be helpful conversation partners. In the years after my wife's death, I became a bit of a sage on the subject of losing a wife. Several minister friends who suffered the death of a spouse would ask to come by and talk with me. We would sit on the porch or deck and just talk about what it was like to lose a spouse. Often, I was asked a host of questions as if the friend had been waiting with bated breath to talk with me. I didn't have particularly insightful things to say. It was just helpful for those who had lost a spouse to sit with me and share their thoughts and feelings. We laughed, cried, joked, and told serious stories. As they came, so they went—only feeling better as they went. They felt better not because of any bit of wisdom I shared but because friends talking about loss is healing.

Being proactive and setting goals can be very helpful. Grief tends to overwhelm, and those who are having a hard time with it tend to feel out of control—as if grief is in the driver's seat and those who grieve are at the mercy of a crazy process. Setting goals gives a sense that we are in control of our grief. With time, achieving goals gives a sense of real progress in the grief process.

What goals? In the case of the death of a spouse, decide on a time for children to come for a visit and help you go through their parent's things and decide what to keep. Make a decision and set a date to clean out their things from the master bedroom closet. In the case of the death of a child, set a date to begin redecorating the child's room. Granted, few of us will feel like doing these things when the date arrives— you must force yourself to do these things. If you don't set goals to move forward with grief—you will get stuck in the grief process. Moving forward in grief requires making yourself do things you don't want to do. Clearly, you don't want to establish a rash of goals or deadlines and then mechanically get it done. Yet, on the other extreme, if you don't set goals and dates, you may never move forward in grief.

One of the most important aspects of the journey with grief is deciding to move forward with the grief process. The issue might be formed with the question: "Do you want to move through grief and find a 'better place,' or do you want to stay in the quagmire of grief?" You may never find the "better place" unless you are willing to make specific decisions and set specific dates (establishing goals) to facilitate the grief journey.

Now, truth be told, some people don't want to progress with grief to a new, better place. Eric Erickson, the psychologist, identified the last stage of life as making peace with all that has gone before. If a spouse dies after sixty-five years of marriage, the remaining partner may not want to progress in the experience of grief. Staying connected to grief and the one who has gone on ahead may be the way the living spouse decides to give meaning and purpose to the last stage of their life. Moving to a better place is not the goal for everyone; it is the goal for those who choose it.

Reestablishing friendships can be very helpful. Friends tend to struggle to know how to relate to you after a significant loss. A neighbor may be clueless about what to say after your loss. The neighbor will probably not risk saying the wrong thing, so they will hold back around you. It is important for the one experiencing grief to reach out to friends and neighbors to establish a sense of normalcy in relationships. Waiting for others, friends, to reach out, establish a new normal, or reestablish relationships will prove futile. Friends will not risk upsetting you by saying the wrong thing, so they will not generally take the initiative to reestablish the relationship.

Protect yourself from unwise decisions. A great rule of thumb is to not make any significant decisions in the first six months after a significant loss (assuming severe or profound grief). In the introduction of this book, I talked a bit about balance in one's life following grief and loss. Three months into grief, the one grieving is apt to feel as if they have restored balance to their lives; they would be wrong in that assumption. Avoid making significant decisions in the wake of loss. If decisions must be made, a good plan is to bring a trusted family member or friend into the decision-making process. This other person will be able to help you make better decisions.

George Bonanno, sharing the research of others, noted that sadness has a helpful quality in this regard.

> When we experience sadness, our attention turns inward, and we reflect, take stock, and adjust our sense of the world to encompass one in which the person or thing we have lost no longer physically exists . . . When people are made to feel temporarily sad . . . they become more detail-oriented [and make fewer mistakes].[2]

---

2. Bonanno, *Other Side of Sadness*, 45–46.

Engaging in new activities and meeting new people can be helpful. This is especially true for those who have lost a spouse. Before my wife's death, we had an active circle of friends, to the point it sometimes felt as if we shared a hyphenated name, Ron-and-Cyndi. The longer you have been married or together, the more you feel as if you have lost part of yourself in the death of your spouse.

Earlier this morning, I was waiting in a lounge area for a small repair on my car to be completed. When my name was called, I went to the desk to pay the bill and retrieve my keys. As I was leaving, a gentleman my age approached me and said, "Your cell phone slipped out of your pocket while you were seated." I took my phone and thanked him for being so thoughtful. That is when he said, "Yeah, it is hard to get through a day without your cell phone."

It is tough when you lose the other part of your hyphenated self. It is also difficult for friends who thought of you as hyphenated. Following the death of a spouse, your friends will try very hard to find a new normal in the relationship you share with them; the more hyphenated you were, the harder the struggle will be for them and you. While that hyphenated shared history with your friends is rich and wonderful, it can also be a kind of baggage dragged around—following you everywhere.

Being patient and kind with yourself is critical on the journey through grief. Mental fog, maybe not enough sleep, too many decisions to make too quickly—all of this can be a recipe for being impatient and unkind to yourself. The discomfort, struggle, and pain of the journey through grief can be frustrating and disheartening. All of us who grieve want to take giant steps when we only seem able to manage baby steps. Accept and learn to give thanks for baby steps.

The alternative is to be impatient and unkind to yourself: this would be profoundly counterproductive. Those who are impatient and unkind to themselves in the journey of grief make the journey much harder than it needs to be.

An insight from Bonanno's research will be helpful here. His research is based on self-reporting by individuals. That is, research subjects are asked a series of questions, and conclusions are drawn from scrutinizing the data from those interviews or researchers' observations. Bonanno's research,[3] and that of others,[4] identified two key psychological characteristics that helped people cope effectively with sadness and grief: flexibility and optimism. Two observations are important.

Flexibility and optimism are dispositional characteristics often associated with one's personality. Some people are by nature flexible and/or optimistic. In Bonanno's research, people who identify as flexible and optimistic coped better with sadness and grief than those who did not identify with these terms.

Regardless of how we might identify with these terms, in processing grief, those who practice flexibility and optimism will cope better with sadness and grief. How might this work itself out amid processing grief? People who might identify as less than fully flexible, at times, simply have "gone with the flow." An example may help. When I visit with my adult children and grandchildren, we occasionally go out to dinner at one of their favorite restaurants. When the grandchildren were very young, these places tended to be places the kids liked. Now that the grandchildren are older, it tends to be restaurants my children prefer. And my preference? I "go with the flow." My children and grandchildren tend to prefer restaurants that would not be at the top of my list of

---

3. Ibid., 113–14.

4. C. S. Carver, M. F. Scheier, and S. C. Segerstrom, "Optimism," *Clinical Psychology Review* 30 (2010): 879–89.

favorite places. When they are choosing the restaurant, I go with the flow because, for me, doing something with family is the chief priority, not dietary considerations.

When processing grief, "go with the flow." If one insists on a less than flexible approach, sadness and grief will be much more difficult and much longer. The priority is getting through grief, not experiencing grief according to a preordained pattern. Flexibility in the days, weeks, months and years after a significant loss will pay great dividends.

In a similar way, viewing the present and future through an optimistic lens will also greatly aid in the processing of grief. For those who are not optimistic by nature, this will require a little self-monitoring and self-discipline. Self-monitoring is when you realize you are being less than optimistic. Self-discipline is when you decide to set aside the well-worn, unoptimistic perspective and embrace a more hopeful view of the present and future. One's optimism can grow if progress can be identified; thus, there is a need to establish simple, achievable goals in the journey through grief.

Any way you frame the conversation, sadness and grief are difficult. It will be easier if flexibility and optimism are your friends.

Bonanno's research also identified a few positive factors that were associated with better outcomes in the process of grieving. Most of these are almost self-evident: better financial resources, better education, better physical health, fewer ongoing life stressors to worry about, and a broader network of friends and family to help in the ongoing process of grieving.[5]

---

5. Bonanno, *Other Side of Sadness*, 110.

Chapter 7

Grief and Positive Emotions

I developed rather strong opinions about death and grief over the twenty-seven years I regularly walked with parishioners through their grief. One of them might be stated as, "Grief is important work, but there comes a time when you just need to throw a party." While it might seem a bit callous to my readers, my wife and I had a saying related to the possibility that one of us might end up on a ventilator: there comes a time when you just have to pull the plug and throw a party.

This sense of a party being an appropriate response to a death grew slowly out of my experience with grieving families. Some of the most enthusiastic laughter I have ever experienced came during funeral services. In the midst of grief, some attend funeral services with a pent-up need to laugh. I made it a point to try to invite funeral attendees to laugh; I often did this by telling a funny story about the deceased. I was always impressed by the robust laughter I received during the funeral service. Obviously, this is not true in the most traumatic of circumstances, the death of a child or teenager. Even so, most people will be significantly surprised to know that laughter at a funeral is one of the most cleansing things one will ever experience.

I think this same sentiment might be behind the increasing interest in celebration of life services as opposed to traditional funerals.

In the days after the sudden death of my wife, my children reminded me of our family saying: "Grieve but throw a party." In the case of my wife, we held two memorial services. One was a few days after her death in Richmond, Virginia (where we lived at the time of her death), and the second was a few days after that in Orlando, Florida (where we had many friends from our pastoral years there). In conjunction with the Orlando funeral, we decided to rent a house near Disney and spend a few days dedicated to having fun following the Orlando service.

So, three generations, all thirteen of us, gathered for three days at Disney and Universal. Hear me when I say this was one of the best decisions I made in the wake of my wife's death. Those three days of fun together were priceless. Those few days at Disney and Universal began a tradition in our family. Every year, we take a family trip, largely funded by an IRA I inherited from my wife. We spend 'her money' on these trips—and she would have approved a thousand times over. We are now in our seventh year of this tradition. As I write this, we are packing for a trip to St. John, USVI. These have been immensely healing events. It has allowed my granddaughters to see parts of the world they may not have seen for many decades.

In an earlier chapter, I wrote about differing grief traditions in religious traditions. One of the key similarities in those traditions was the focus on sadness and respect for the deceased. Ingrained in Western Civilization is this heavy note that grief centers on sadness and sorrow. While I would never suggest that sadness and sorrow are not essential parts of grief, I do want to suggest that emotionally uplifting experiences can also be essential in moving forward with grief.

Modern research on bereavement is also raising questions about our potential overemphasis on sadness and sorrow in grief. Research by Melissa Soenke and Jeff Greenberg[1] noted that positive emotions (going to a party or watching entertainment) were more effective in reducing sadness and grief than negative emotions (confronting grief, talking with family about the deceased, journaling, etc.). Experiences that lift emotions are more beneficial to those grieving than those traditionally associated with grief work.[2]

My own grief experience confirmed this reality. In the weeks after my wife's death, I began declining to meet with friends for coffee or lunch. Of course, my friends were interested in supporting and helping me in my grief. From my perspective, I came to realize their best intentions had the net effect of pulling me back into the ditch of sorrow. My friends were not helping me on my journey with grief; they were unknowingly holding me down in the pit of despair. All my friends tended to want to talk about my grief, my sadness. They asked how the kids were dealing with her death, and, of course, there were all the heartfelt expressions of sympathy that tended to confirm I ought to be having a tough time with my grief—even when I was having a rare good day.

Out of many thoughtful meetings with friends, no one asked, "So, I know you follow the NBA; who do you think will make the playoffs?" Or "You remember that crazy convention trip we took—was that eighteen years ago?" No one commented on current events. No one treated me as 'normal.' Almost instinctively, too many of my friends assumed getting me to recite again the events of her death was somehow going to help me. At times, I wondered if they wanted me to help them with their curiosity about the circumstances around my wife's death. Granted, finding your

---

1. O'Connor, *Grieving Brain*, 135–37.
2. Bonanno, *Other Side of Sadness*, 54–59.

wife on the floor dead is probably not typical, and maybe it does provoke curiosity.

In the months after my wife's death, I found myself going out to breakfast more often. It was nice being around and among people who assumed I was off to the start of a good day. In places where I was a stranger, no one seemed alarmed that I appeared happy and upbeat.

In 1999, psychologists Margaret Stroebe and Henk Schut developed the dual process model of coping with bereavement. Professional bereavement counselors frequently use this model. The researchers identify two categories of experiences in the everyday lives of those who grieve. Loss-oriented experiences include grief work, denial/avoidance of changes, and day-to-day experiences that illicit a memory of the loss. Restoration-oriented experiences include attending to life changes, doing new things, distracting from grief, and developing new relationships. The key insight in the Stroebe/Schut model is the suggestion that most grieving people oscillate between loss-oriented and restoration-oriented experiences daily, sometimes hourly.[3] Their research confirms that people with anything near normal grief find themselves shifting from loss-oriented experiences to restoration-based experiences daily. This oscillation, up and down emotionally, is well-established among those who grieve. Over time, people spend less time in loss-oriented experiences as they adapt and move forward in their grief.

Based on the Stroebe/Schut model, friends who wanted to help me with my grief were effectively drawing me back toward loss-based experiences when I was trying to move toward restoration-based experiences. My friends, of course, are to be applauded for being concerned for me. They were

---

3. O'Connor, *Grieving Brain*, 76.

caught in the larger culture's near overemphasis on sorrow and sadness in grief.

Research on bereavement has shown that positive emotional experiences help people cope with grief more than what has traditionally been identified as the good work of grief. Throwing a party is a good idea. Those who grieve will benefit from positive, uplifting emotional experiences.

In an earlier chapter about influencers of grief, I noted that Jewish and Islamic traditional perspectives of grief have well-established timeframes for grief. Timeframes for periods of sadness immediately after the loss of a loved one have the additional benefit of permitting life to return to normal when the timeframe is exceeded. There may be ancient wisdom in traditional timeframes for grief and then providing permission for resuming everyday life.

The benefit of emotionally uplifting experiences is essential for those who grieve. Here is one of the points where I invite us to think more strategically about grief. Cultural permission is important in the grieving context. When grieving the loss of a loved one, many people do not have the emotional reserves to challenge their sub-culture's view about appropriate grief. Consequently, if the subculture (formally or informally) suggests that sadness-based grief is to last for a year, then those in this sub-culture who are grieving the loss of a loved one may not have the emotional resources to challenge the subculture's established perspective. In this way, the so-called rule about sadness inhibits individuals' ability to move forward in their grief. As my well-intentioned friends mentioned earlier, the subculture is dragging folks back into the deep ditch of grief when they are trying to move more fully to restoration-oriented activities.

Lest I am misunderstood, I am referring to people experiencing normal grief. Positive emotional experiences have been proven to help people who are grieving. How can we provide greater permission to those in the midst of grief to experience positive emotional events?

Over the years, I have listened to many comments about my family's tradition of taking trips together, which grew out of my wife's death. When I have told people that I am spending my wife's IRA on taking family trips or that we developed the tradition of taking fun family trips in response to her death, the response has always been consistent: "I think that is great. What a wonderful thing to do."

While people say it is "a good thing to do," I don't see other people doing anything similar when their loved one dies. Rather, I see people dutifully following well-established sadness-based perspectives on grief.

Given cultural norms and constraints, it is very difficult for people to give themselves permission to embrace positive emotional experiences as a way to assist in moving forward with grief. Grieving the loss of a loved one and throwing a party are not mutually exclusive, nor are they contradictory.

Because of the sudden death of my wife, it took a few days for my family and extended family to gather. As a family, then and now, we are in four different states.

I appreciated that my family understood the need to give me space and support me when needed. I never felt crowded. I was never treated as emotionally damaged. My children gently helped me when decisions were hard to make and supported my decisions in the immediate aftermath of their mother's death. The environment I sensed in those days after her death might be characterized by, "Give him some space. He can feel and think whatever he wants to feel and think. He just lost his wife."

My son's father-in-law mowed my grass, and my other son's mother-in-law was in the house and helpful at every turn. I now know my children made a host of necessary decisions in those days, yet they discussed all the big decisions

with me. I made those decisions, and the children imple-
mented them.

Looking back over those days, maybe the best part of it
was my children and extended family had no expectations
about the nature or shape of my grief. Immediately after the
death of a spouse, when your brain is in a major fog, the last
thing you need is someone telling you or implying there is a
right way to grieve.

In the days after my wife's death, with a house full of family,
there were times I needed to be alone with my thoughts. In
those moments, I would wander out on the deck in the back
yard or slip off into the formal living room, which was almost
always empty. On those occasions, I noticed supportive eyes
from time to time checking on me without intruding.

I was also aware and appreciative of how my extended
family supported the youngest of the grandchildren. Three of
my granddaughters are six to eight years older than the three
younger ones; thus, we refer to the "littles" and the "bigs." At
the time of my wife's death, the "littles" were six, six, and four.
Children of that age sometimes struggle to know how to react
to the death of a family member. Often, they just mirror or
reflect the emotions of their parents. I was pleased with how
my children and extended family helped the "littles." There
was no pressure on the "littles" to behave a certain way or
respond in a certain way to their grandmother's death. Plenty
of helpful adults were around to answer questions the "littles"
might have, but there were no expectations about how the
"littles" should act.

On one occasion, I remember sitting alone in the living
room and hearing the "littles" up in a bedroom on the second
floor. Apparently, the girls were playing a game. Two days after
my wife's death, to hear their giggling laughter waft through
the house was like a heavenly choir singing. Their laughter
offered the hope of a happier day for me. It reminded me of

all the laughter our home had experienced over the previous decade and offered the hope that belly laughs might one day return for me.

I have always been interested in how supportive family and friends talk about grief with those in the throes of it. When we see a friend who has suffered loss, we tend to say things like "So, how are you doing?"; "I know this must be a sad time for you"; "I am praying for you"; "I am sorry for your loss." These phrases and others tend to reinforce the notion that those who grieve should feel sad and are in need of being cared for.

Caring professionals and those who see themselves as persons on a mission to care for others must be careful in how they respond to those who grieve. It is easy for those committed to caring for others to fall into an unfortunate cycle: Please, I need you to act helpless so I can fulfill my mission of compassionate care. Sometimes, the language we use and the nonverbal communication we offer can send an unintended message: I will give you more attention if you play the part of being emotionally damaged.

In American culture, there seems to be plenty of sympathy for those who suffer loss; I wish we could develop a little more expectation that those who grieve are fully capable of managing their sorrow. In moments of grief, I wish everyone could hear the gentle laughter of children upstairs, as life was once full of positive emotions and thoughts, so it will be again. Helping those who grieve to experience positive, uplifting, emotional events will help them move through their grief.

Everyone needs to see a little light at the end of the tunnel.

Chapter 8

Finding and Celebrating a New Normal

In the classic thriller *The Silence of the Lambs*, FBI trainee Clarice Starling searches for a serial killer. Late in the movie, she figures out that the serial killer knew his first victim, Frederica Bimmel. Starling travels to Bimmel's home to interview her mother and asks if she could see the teenager's bedroom. Upstairs, the mother opens the teenager's bedroom and notes that the room is exactly as it was when her daughter disappeared.

For the viewer, the note that the bedroom has not been changed is one more creepy fact in a movie filled with creepiness at every turn. Yet, the viewer intuitively knows that if the room is "exactly as it was" when the daughter died, then the parents are struggling with moving on from their grief. The teenager's room has become a memorial, a constant reminder of the family's terrible loss.

Stability and continuity can be a source of comfort and security in the wake of a terrible loss, but attempting to keep everything "exactly as it was" is a recipe for troublesome grief. After a significant loss, everything is different: you become the widow/widower, the parent who lost a child. You walk into the little diner where you have eaten breakfast every Sunday morning for the last six months, and the regulars look at you differently. The folks in the book club treat you differently for your loss. Friends don't quite know what to do with you.

My wife and I were participants in a small dinner group when we lived in Orlando, Florida. The five couples shared dinner one night a month (except in the summer). We dropped out of the dinner group when we moved from Orlando to Richmond. After her death, I was back in Orlando for a visit, and the group decided to get together for dinner; it was the first time we gathered after my wife's death. It was awkward, especially when it came to where people would sit around the table.

Things are just different after a significant loss. There is no real going back to the way things were before the loss. Deciding what to keep and what to let go of is part of moving forward after a loss.

On of the myths associated with grief is that those experiencing grief will, at some point, get back to themselves. That is, after the experience of grief we return to being our "old selves." Grief, especially severe and profound grief, forever changes us. We don't go back to being the old self, rather we find a new and different normal.

The death of a loved one is not something we get over. Seven years removed from the death of my wife, I still miss her and have moments when I grieve her death. Losing a significant person in our lives is not something we will ever get over. It, rather, is something we learn to live with.

I am going to offer advice around several ideas.

Decide what you will keep.

Keep only the things you absolutely cannot part with.

Three months after my wife's death, my children came back to help me go through her things and give things away to a worthy cause. Soon after the funeral, we scheduled their visit: I initiated setting the date as I knew it was a critical step in moving forward with grief.

A week before their arrival, I spent a day looking through my wife's things and making peace with what was about to unfold with the arrival of my children. I remember sitting in a folding chair in our shared bedroom closet, looking at the racks of clothes and shoes my wife had worn. I recalled when she wore a few items that were tied to special events in our lives, including her wedding gown and golf outfits. I suspect I was embracing memories in the closet for an hour and a half.

Two things helped me let go of her things in our closet. One was the awareness if I really wanted to move forward with my grief, I *needed* to let go of her things. Second was the sense that donating to a worthy cause meant another person would wear her things and make a new memory, maybe a precious memory. And so, I let go of her things in our shared closet.

I had a similar sense about her jewelry, except my daughter divided most of it into bags for our grandchildren. I did keep her engagement ring and wedding band.

I think most grieving people have trouble letting go of things after the death of a loved one. After losing someone significant, there is a near primal need to hold on to everything related to the one who died. I know that feeling well. In the midst of deep feelings, it is important to recognize that the more you hold onto, the longer you are making the journey with intense grief.

Decide what you will abandon or let go of.

When we suffer a significant loss, there is always part of us that yearns to turn back the clock before the loss. We imagine that if we can just keep things the same, that in some way honors the deceased loved one. After the death of a spouse or child, trying to go back and keep everything as it was before the loss is fraught with challenges.

Over forty-two years of marriage, we collected boxes of decorative Santas. We loved to display them during the Christmas holidays. After her death, I wondered what I would do with the Santas, dozens of them.

My initial thought was I would keep them all and display them during the Christmas holidays year after year. On second reflection, I realized holding on to them would, in effect, be a way of holding on to my deceased wife. While holding on to the full collection of Santas was appealing, I recognized it could well thwart my best efforts at moving forward with my grief.

I displayed all the Santas (during June 2016) in the spare bedroom. Occasionally I would walk into the room and just look at them. In time I identified two basic categories of Santas. One group I had a particular affinity to as they were Santas I especially liked. The other group was Santas that I had no particular affinity to and could easily part with.

Then, I went back to the first group, the ones I wanted to keep, and asked the question, "Are these Santas I have to keep for myself, or are they Santas I would be delighted to see in the homes of my children?" In time, I divided the first group into those I had to hold on to and those I would love to see in my children's home. Thus, I divided that first grouping into two groups—which would be kept in either my home or the homes of my children.

Upon a bit more reflection, I asked myself another question, "If one of my children or grandchildren really wanted a particular Santa, even if it was one I had identified I wanted to keep, would I give it to them?"

I am describing above the elaborate process I went through to deal with the collection of Santas. In the end, I took pictures of all the Santas and posted them for my children to go through and pick the ones they wanted. I did not reserve any exclusively for myself.

The disposition of the Santas was a big deal for me. I recognized that holding onto them was, in effect, holding on to my deceased wife. If I kept all of them, it was going to be more difficult and time-consuming for me to move through my grief. In some ways, the decision about the Santas was a decision to either live in the afterglow of my marital relationship or to move forward with my grief and find a new and, for me, healthier normal.

If you cannot abandon things, you will struggle with moving forward with and grief to a better place.

Another example maybe helpful.

In our last years together, we had begun our search for a new place to live in retirement. The search had been narrowed to Central Florida, outside Myrtle Beach, or, of all places, Columbia, South Carolina. My wife was driving the retirement bus, and her love of golf was front and center. After her death and before my retirement, I needed to finalize plans for where I would live in retirement.

I didn't want to continue to live in the Mechanicsville home we shared for nearly ten years; in truth, it was much larger than I wanted and needed. Staying in the Richmond area would have been a possibility, but I was interested in warmer weather and easier access to southern locations for travel. Following through on one of the three locations we had identified above was a possibility, but I thought better of it as those locations were a bit isolated from my support system, and life in those locations would always reflect, to some degree, my wife's fascination with golf.

The decision about where to live in retirement was one heavily influenced by the search my wife and I had conducted over several years. If I wanted to move forward with my grief to a better place, I needed to choose a location that was representative of my new normal and its future.

Another example. After my wife's death, I gave up golf. Prior to her death, 95 percent of the golf I played was with her. It was our thing. After her death, I tried playing golf on two occasions. I quickly discovered that playing golf was dominated by memories of all the times I played with her; I couldn't "keep my head in the game" because of all the memories intruding. In retrospect, I probably could have worked through those thoughts and feelings tied to golf if I had worked at it. It wasn't worth the effort for me.

As I know you want to know, my children selected some of my favorite Santas, ones I had planned on keeping for myself. It was the wiser decision to allow them to choose. I cannot describe the pride and pleasure I feel when I visit their homes and see my old Santa pals! Knowing that my grandchildren will find joy in them is nothing short of priceless.

You must let go of some things if you truly want to move forward with grief to a better place. You must let go of some things that are very meaningful to you.

Try new activities.

We all are familiar with the old saying, "The definition of insanity is doing the same thing over again and expecting different results."

A new normal will require new activities.

I noted in a previous chapter my friends' efforts to be supportive of me in my loss ended up pulling me backward in my moving forward with grief. If you go back to all the things you were doing before the death of your loved one, then moving forward with grief is going to be more difficult. Inevitably, you will get locked into the old framework and become limited in your ability to move forward.

Because of the social framework prior to your loss, you may be known in the future as your spouse's widow or widower or as the parents who lost a son, etc. These social frameworks will tend to keep you locked into a particular way of seeing yourself.

New activities will facilitate moving to a new normal.

Significant loss is a time to think of things you always wanted to do, but never did. It is a great time to take up hiking, or biking, or boating. It is a good time to get in the swing of pickleball, or join the gym, or join a book club.

Build new relationships.

Building new relationships helps us move through and beyond grief.

As I indicated earlier, I decided not to pursue potential retirement locations in the golf destinations my wife and I had been looking at prior to her death. Nor did I decide to stay in the home where we lived before her death; it was much larger than I needed and carried too many memories. I also decided against living near my children. This was a difficult decision as my children all wanted me to move close to them. I knew if I did move close to one of them, they would probably end up taking me under their wing. I did not want that for them. In my pastoral life, I had seen that happen too many times, and it rarely ended well for anyone.

As I had lived for many years in the Richmond, Virginia, area, I decided to look for a new home in the larger metro area. Completely unplanned, I fell in love with a fixer-upper in Powhatan County. Never in my wildest imagination did I ever think I would retire and move to the country. The home

I eventually bought met several needs for me. As a lifelong DIY guy, I knew a project would be good for me. The house I decided on had been pretty much neglected for the previous five years because the older couple living there was no longer physically able to manage the property. I spent the first two years of my retirement working on the property, getting the house, shrubs, and flower beds back in good shape. Along the way, I embraced a few projects: rebuilding rock wall terracing in the backyard and replacing an ugly, exposed clay hillside with a regraded shrub and flower bed. I love those butterfly bushes. In year three, I replaced the boards on the deck. Every year, I have undertaken painting projects on the exterior of the house.

The location of the house just outside Richmond, Virginia, kept me relatively close to the host of friends I had developed over the previous decade; many of whom are ministerial friends.

The relatively small neighborhood was also a draw for me. There are forty-nine homes in the development with an active community: lots of people enjoy walking at various times during the day. It is a small enough community where neighbors can keep up with and help one another. I quickly made new friends. In a community this small, folks are always interested in the new people who move into the neighborhood. As I was open to new relationships with neighbors, it was easy to meet neighbors.

Rodney and Mark are probably the neighbors closest to me. Rodney is a retired physical therapist who offers great advice when I do more than I should in the yard. Mark is a retired parts store manager. Across the pond from where I live is Wilma. She is a University of North Carolina fan; as I am a North Carolina State University graduate, we text back and forth in the fall about how our schools are doing in basketball. Across the street from my driveway, Helen and

Doug live. He is retired from the military and has traveled all over the world. They met when he was on duty in London; she is British, has a delightful accent, and is a chef. Just down the street are Matt and Amy; they are a blended family and decided on a new start in Powhatan. Bill and Linda are of Norwegian descent and live down the street across from Wilma; when I host a neighborhood party, she brings the most interesting desserts! These are my new neighbors and now friends.

Through a friend who lives on our street, I became interested in the Free Clinic of Powhatan and have volunteered at various times.

These are new friends who have come into my life since my wife's death; I consider myself very fortunate in the friend department. I have made these new friends while hanging on to friends I have known for forty years. The new friends have helped me move forward with grief—though I have never said that to them. They don't think of me as the guy whose wife died. They think of me as the DIY guy who lives at 2975. Old friends are like mile markers in the past; they provide stability and continuity. New friends help us embrace a new future.

Most people who suffer grief do not relocate. In that setting, friendships might shift a bit in the years after the death of a spouse. People who find themselves single may also gravitate toward other single adults in their larger group of friends, especially those who have lost a spouse.

Building new relationships or reinvigorating old friendships is very important in finding a new normal.

Take on new causes.

Join a pickleball group, along with everyone else in the universe. Pickleball is a popular and exploding pastime for many people, especially seniors. Catching this cultural wave is an easy way to find new friends and take on new interests.

Find a new place to volunteer. Sometimes this will center in a special interest you have always had but never fulfilled. The death of a loved one can open that door. Sometimes, this involves simply become more active in something you have always been involved in, like your religious community.

'Taking on a new cause' might also involve your career. Plenty of people reevaluate their careers in the wake of a significant death and decide on a slightly different career path going forward. This can open new interests and causes going forward.

Others create a new pathway forward related to their loss. Mothers Against Drunk Drivers (MADD) is an organization literally created by moms who lost a child to a drunk driver's accident. The danger is that MADD moms might be tempted to remain mad about the death of their child. And surely, some parents do funnel their anger at loss into worthy causes. In time, their volunteer efforts help them make some measure of peace with their loss, and in the meantime, they are about important work—raising awareness about drinking and driving.

Sometimes, it is helpful to do something constructive with the energy of loss and grief.

My readers may remember Naomi, who lost her daughter in the Fukushima tsunami. When she could not find her daughter, she trained on earth-moving equipment and went digging to find her. Of course, her daughter was eventually found, and she stopped digging. Let's pick up that story again.

And so, in April 2013, Naomi found herself back in the classroom, at the Kanan West Junior High School in Ishinomaki. It was two years since the disaster. "My class was a ninth-grade class," she said. "In other words, they were Koharu's class." Every time she looked up from her desk, Naomi faced children exactly the same age that her daughter would have been, if she had survived . . . .[1]

Naomi continued to work at the school where Koharu would have attended. It was therapy. It was an opportunity to invest in children in the community. She taught, and mothered, them all.

---

1. Richard Lloyd Parry, *Ghosts of the Tsunami*, 208.

Conclusion

Last year I became certified as a scuba diver. This past March, I dove with my two sons for the first time off the Florida Keys. It was a priceless experience.

Prior to becoming certified, I read everything I could about scuba diving. I watched dozens of YouTube videos about recreational diving. When I began the certification process, I had a head filled with cargo about theoretical diving. The five dives in a local pool were very helpful in gaining confidence in some of the critical skills necessary for diving.

Then, I completed my certification in a quarry in 58-degree water with very low visibility. In cold water, thirty feet down, it's hard to hold natural panic at bay.

Let me illustrate. A key scuba skill is the ability to clear your mask. If, while on a dive, your mask comes loose and fills with water, the diver must know how to clear the mask of water. This is an essential skill for the scuba diver. Practicing the skill is straightforward: beneath the surface, a diver takes off their mask, replaces the mask, and clears the mask. Clearing the mask requires the diver to press on the top of the mask, press the mask to their forehead, tilt the head back, and then vigorously blow through the nose, filling the mask with air and chasing the water out of the mask. Sometimes, it may require blowing air out of their nose twice. This process is almost fail-proof if practiced correctly.

I did this several times without difficulty in a local pool on the weekend of my five dives. Of course, in 58-degree murky quarry water, it is a very different experience. In the quarry, I took the mask off easily, put it back on, pressed the top of the mask against my forehead, and tilted my head back—and then something went terribly wrong, and I was not able to clear the mask. I immediately swam to the surface, coughing and spitting water. I was in a bit of a panic. The instructor shortly swam up to the surface and calmly asked what happened. I wasn't sure. The instructor patiently told me that I did everything perfectly right, except that instead of blowing through my nose, I blew air out my mouth and into the regulator. I had done everything right except I didn't breathe through my nose—thus, my failure. In stressed circumstances, simple tasks can become very complex and difficult.

As a pastor, I walked with several hundred families through their grief and witnessed how stressed circumstances made the journey more difficult. In addition, in my professional capacity, I kept up with the literature about death, dying, and grief. My professional life offered me a lot of experience with grief. I found my own grief offered nuances and insights I could never have gained except by traveling the road of grief myself. Like my struggle with clearing the scuba mask, it is hard to appreciate some difficulties until you are in a stressful situation yourself. My own experience of grief has been a re-education for me. Of course, those who have never been emotionally wrung out by severe or profound grief have insights to share. I am all for learning about grief in any way you can. Even so, my own experience of grief has provided significant insight for me and created in me an urgency to articulate a healthier image of grief. Most of what is available on the internet and in the general culture of our day is inadequate and can complicate grief for individuals.

In writing this book, I hope that I have accomplished several things.

I hope this book will help the efforts of many others in finally putting aside the unhelpful notion that there are five stages to grief, that there is a recommended pathway with grief, and that individuals can get past grief. Cultural expectations around grief are greatly increasing the struggle of grief for many, needlessly and pointlessly.

I hope this book will provide some insight to those on a lonely pathway through grief. Getting clear information about what is happening in the grieving process provides a little light at the end of the tunnel.

I hope this book will assist the larger conversation about the nature of grief. In articulating the tsunami image, I am providing a new and different way to think about grief, a pathway appreciative of the new science of bereavement. As this science is in its infancy, we are presented with a unique opportunity to join hands and significantly expand our understanding and appreciation of grief. Everyone has a contribution to make to this larger conversation about grief as long as we see it as a dialogue, not a monologue. Each worldview and faith perspective has a contribution to make to enrich the overall conversation.

Some of my readers will remember the overnight sensation *Who Moved My Cheese?* by Spencer Johnson and Kenneth Blanchard, published in 2011. The book illustrated resistance in the workplace to change with mice trapped in a maze searching for cheese; thus, the panic phrase, "Who moved my cheese?" Deepak Malhotra wrote a lesser-known response to the Johnson/Blanchard book, published in January 2013, titled *I Moved Your Cheese: For Those Who Refuse to Live as*

Mice in Someone Else's Maze.[1] The Malhotra book is deeply philosophical and raises questions about why we would think of office employees as mice in the first place.

The key character in the book is a mouse named Max. Initially, Max embraced his life in the maze. He, too, spent time racing around looking for cheese, which seemed to appear in different places in the maze at different times. While all the other mice seemed content to simply chase the cheese, Max began to ask questions: Why does the location of the cheese change? Who is providing the cheese? Why this maze? Can I get out of the maze? In time, Max did just that; he escaped the maze and learned the maze was in a university lab. Every day, a professor visited the lab to check on his mice experiment and left detailed written instructions for graduate students. The graduate students arrived later and simply followed the instructions provided by the professor.

Max hatched a plan. After the professor left the lab, Max rewrote the instructions to provide a larger quantity of cheese to the mice in the maze. When the graduate students arrived, they followed Max's instructions, assuming they were the professor's instructions. In time, Max grew bored with tricking the graduate students and fooling the professor.

Max returned in hopes of liberating the other mice in the maze. Max explained that the maze was an artificial world controlled by a professor and graduate students. Max offered to help the other mice escape. The other mice laughed at Max. They thought he had lost his mind. The other mice continued to live in the maze and ran around looking for cheese.

Toward the end of the book Max met Zed, a master wizard who knew the truth about the university lab, professor and

---

1. Deepak Malhotra, *I Moved Your Cheese: For Those Who Refuse to Live as Mice in Someone Else's Maze* (San Francisco: Barrett-Koehler, 2011), 25.

graduate students. Max shared his frustration the other mice lived within the constraints of the maze and were unwilling to question the status quo.

"Zed smiled. 'You see, Max, the problem is not that the mouse is in the maze, but that the maze is in the mouse.'"[2]

The biggest obstacle to healthy grieving is the maze in us; we have embraced outdated and false ideas about grief and loss. We have listened too long and too intensely to special interests and to the priorities of self-interested entrepreneurs. We have wandered from faith traditions and their tried-and-true pathways through grief; consequently, when it is our turn to grieve, we grab for almost anything available if we think it will help. The complexity of modern life has not helped either.

I invite my readers to remember the long legacy of death and grief in our species; for tens of thousands of years we seemed to manage grief. The maze in us makes grief harder than it needs to be, we spend way "too much time in our own heads." Healthy grieving calls us to dispense with the maze inside ourselves and embrace a deeper and healthier perspective on grief.

All the best for you on your journey.

2. Ibid.

About the Author

Ron Crawford is a retired minister living in Powhatan County, Virginia. He was president and professor of pastoral ministry at Baptist Theological Seminary at Richmond (Virginia) for ten years before his retirement in 2017. In that capacity, he taught courses in pastoral theology and practice, focusing on twenty-first-century social trends and the Church's response to them.

His twenty-seven-year pastoral experience includes pastorates in Danville and Richmond, Virginia; Asheville, North Carolina; and Orlando, Florida.

He holds degrees from North Carolina State University (BA in history and philosophy), Southeastern Baptist Theological Seminary (MDiv and a DMin in the history and theology of Christian worship), and Virginia Commonwealth University (master's degree in public administration).

He has been active in Baptist circles, serving on the Coordinating Council of the Cooperative Baptist Fellowship, as first vice president, and, later, as president of the Baptist General Association of Virginia.

His previous books include *Finding Love Later in Life: Brunch at the Crooked Oak Café* (2023) and *Towel and Basin Memoir: Personal Reflections on Baptist Theological Seminary at Richmond* (co-editor, 2019). His next project is a manuscript of the history of Baptist Theological Seminary at Richmond, forthcoming in early 2025.

In addition to writing, he enjoys keeping up with current affairs, woodworking, working in his yard, and traveling.